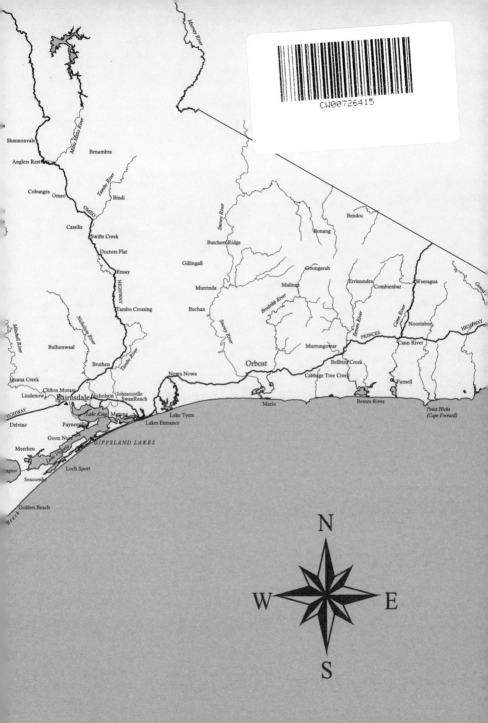

STRAIT

Colourful Tales OF OLD GIPPSLAND

JOHN WELLS

Also by John Wells:

The Mongrel (Macmillan's Orbit Series)
The Mary (Macmillan s Orbit Series)
The City of Berwick Sketchbook
More Colourful Tales of Old Gippsland

National Library of Australia
Cataloguing-in-Publication entry

Wells, John Carlyle, 1945 -
  Colourful Tales of Old Gippsland

  ISBN 0 949449 09 1

1. Gippsland, Victoria-History. I. Title.

994.5
Copyright © John Carlyle Wells.
First published in 1977 by Rigby Ltd

Published in 1984 and 1990 by Landmark Press
2-4Calway Street, Drouin, 3818, Victoria

Reprinted 2003 by Landmark Press

Printed by Shannon Books, Melbourne.

ALSO IN THIS SERIES...

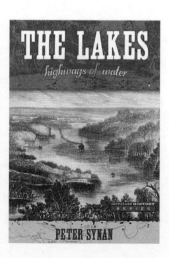

CONTENTS

LIST OF ILLUSTRATIONS

Acknowledgments

It is impossible for me to list the names of all the people who have assisted in this task and I apologise to anyone I have overlooked. Names which I do remember are those of Erle Matthies, 'Bumper' Gee, Mrs Jeanes, Marie Nation, Jack Nobelius, Pat Sweeney, Jean Richards, Ted Mott, the Ure family, the Gregorys, the Hanleys, Evan Henry, Peter Farrago, Mary Dillon, Noel Dyson, the Pennycuicks, Malcolm Studd, Bob Durling, Harold Keys, my brother Euan and my mother, Muriel Bloomer.

I must also acknowledge the help given in various ways by the Australian Railways Historical Society, the State Electricity Commission, the Country Roads Board, General Motors Holden, the Victorian Railways, the Berwick Mechanics Institute Free Library, the Warragul and Wonthaggi Historical Societies, the various centenary committees and the *Age* suburban publications, particularly the always helpful staff of the *West Gippslander*.

I have drawn material from a number of books. Among them were several by Joseph White—*100 Years of History, Poowong—The First Thirty Years*, and *Krowera*; as well there were *An illustrated Guide to the Beaconsfield Ranges, Vision and Realisation*, published by the Victorian Education Department; Neil Gunson's *The Good Country, The Changing Years*, edited by Marie Nation; K. M. Bowden's *The Great Southern Railway*; Raymond Paull's *Old Walhalla*; *The Mirboo and Morwell Railway* by Bob Whitehead; Hugh Copeland's *The Path of Progress*; W. J. Cuthill's *The River of Little Fish*; J. W. Gliddon's *Phillip Island*; J. K. Loney's *Wrecks Along the Gippsland Coast*; and *Glenmaggie 1875—1975* by Betty Chester and Margaret Murphy.

I must also thank all those people who have contacted me with information. Finally I must thank my wife, who has given up much of her own heavily-committed time to make this project a possibility.

For my father and for Joe Doolan

1 The Trains Get Through— Oakleigh to Sale in Only a Day

The Gippsland Railway from Melbourne to Orbost was a vital development for many reasons. It was vital to me because I fell into a deep waterhole excavated by the contractors and nearly drowned. It was also important to me because I was only a child when the line was duplicated and it was all one big adventure to us children. The workmen would often run us to school on their trolleys if we were running late. I also got 'the cuts' from Hec Moir at Longwarry State School when Joe Prout, the ganger on the line, reported me for playing in the sub-station yard.

There were other reasons for its importance, of course. In the late nineteenth century no country area could develop without a railway and Gippsland did not have one. In 1868 the nearest railway station to Gippsland was in Windsor. That wasn't much use to a Gippsland farmer and, as the goldfields petered out, there were more and more farmers in the province. The farmers wanted transport to the Melbourne markets for their produce. Their wives wanted to feel that the 'civilised world' was not too far away. Agitation for a railway began to grow. Sir Charles Gavan Duffy, representing the area in Parliament, joined the fight.

In 1874 the Railway Construction Bill was passed and so began the strangest story of railway building the young country had ever seen. Parliament bickered for months over the route the line would take through Melbourne's suburbs. There was agreement that the line should come through Oakleigh so it was decided to begin from there and sort out the metropolitan end at some later date.

Construction began simultaneously at Oakleigh and at Sale. Work progressed fairly well. There were few of the problems that faced the builders of the South Gippsland line. The Sale-Morwell section was completed by 1 June 1877. On 10 October of that year the Oakleigh-Bunyip section was ready.

What railwaymen called 'The Gap', between Bunyip and Morwell, was bridged by coach. The coach trip became a little shorter in December when the Moe-Morwell section was opened. In March of 1878 'The Gap' disappeared altogether when Moe and Bunyip were joined by rail, but it was not until April of 1879 that the line was extended from Oakleigh to South Yarra.

In South Yarra the railway joined the old line to Princes Bridge. This section had belonged to the Hobson's Bay Railway Company, one of several private companies which once operated railways in Victoria. The Hobson's Bay Railway Company was bought out by the Government of the day.

So by 1878 passengers could travel in comparative comfort from Oakleigh to Sale in the one short day — though they were advised to wear old clothes because of the damage caused by cinders. It is not hard to imagine just what a boon this line must have been to the lonely settlers of Gippsland.

The Argus reported the official opening of the Oakleigh-to-Sale section on 7 March 1878. A special train with 300 dignitaries aboard left Oakleigh at 8.00 a.m. and arrived in Sale only five hours later. The train was greeted in Sale by the firing of salutes, cheering crowds and a huge banquet.

All the contracts for the building of the line were satisfactorily completed, an unusual fact in itself. The Sale-Morwell section was completed on time by Messrs Millar and James. They built sixty-two kilometres of track for £140,499. The Bunyip-Moe and the Moe-Morwell sections were built by the Noonan brothers, who were paid £101 750 for sixty-six kilometres of track. Neil MacNeil secured the initial contract for the Oakleigh-Bunyip section but transferred it to James Leggatt. The contract price for the sixty-two kilometres of track was £101 375. It is hard, now, to imagine Bunyip as a busy rail terminus but for a time that is exactly what is was.

The total cost of the line, including the heavy compensation paid to landowners along the Oakleigh-South Yarra route, was £757,327. Though the problems were less severe in constructing this line than they were in several other cases, there were significant difficulties. Clearing was an expensive process. One tree felled in the Warragul yards was reported by Ebenezer Black McTaggart to be 110 metres long. (This McTaggart was the first station master at Warragul. He had a 'small shack' just over four metres square, for his residence and an even smaller shack for his office.)

The contractors had the problem of moving their locomotives into position. Millar and James had two engines delivered to Sale by ship, with the first, the *St Kilda*, being shipped on the flat-bottomed coaster *Warhawk*, one of the few boats large enough to carry a locomotive and yet able to cross the bar at Lakes Entrance. The *St Kilda* was unloaded at the old wharf below the swing bridge at Sale. The remains of this wharf could be seen until a few years ago. The engine was then towed to Sale on a bullock wagon, with a second wagon carrying the wheels.

The second locomotive, the *Rosedale*, was unloaded at the same place. It was moved to Sale under its own steam, using two sets of tracks. One set was laid in front of the locomotive, which then moved forward while the second set of rails were being moved into position. Once it was on the second set the first lengths of rails were moved around to the front and the process was repeated. It must have been a hot and sweaty procession that finally reached Sale.

Another amusing little story came out of the re-routing of the line near Warragul. The line was planned to go well south of Warragul, through the Minnieburn area. This caused some consternation in the infant township that later became Warragul, so a dinner was given for the planners. The dinner was 'very convivial' and the route was changed to go through Warragul!

In the 1950s the line was duplicated as far as Traralgon and electrified, mainly to speed up the transport of coal and briquettes to Melbourne. The duplication has never been completed. There was no sound foundation available for the new bridge over the Bunyip River and so the section between Bunyip and Longwarry is still a single track and trains must carry a 'staff' to enter it. The staff is transferred back and forth so that no two trains may be in the section at any one time.

The first electric train to use the new track was pulled by locomotive L-1 150, the *George R. Wishart*, the first of the 'L' class locomotives that have become the workhorses of the Gippsland line.

2 Frederick Harris—A Stubborn Man

Like many Scots, Frederick Hamilton Harris was short-tempered and stubborn. Had he not been so, his heart may well have broken.

Harris was of pioneering stock. His father helped open up the Monaro grazing district and his mother was the first white child born on the Coal River, now the Hunter River, the site of today's Newcastle. His grandchildren are still alive and well. That is how close we are to the dawn of our history in this young country. I mean, of course, to the history of the white man here. It is only to him that this old country is a young country.

Frederick Hamilton Harris — and from what I have found out about him, I think that even his wife would have used his full name — spent a long life wrestling with the problems of the land. He married Martha Hamilton, from a sept of his own clan, who came to Australia in 1857. They set up house at Mt Cole, in western Victoria. At that time the area was profitable sheep country.

The Acclimatisation Society had introduced the rabbit to Victoria and these animals were soon to become a national disaster. Despite employing a full-time rabbit shooter, Harris had been eaten out within three years. He sold what was left of his run and moved to Officer, between Berwick and Pakenham.

Everything was loaded onto a bullock dray. His full span of bullocks was Harris's pride and joy; he was so certain of their strength and power that he even allowed (or could not prevent) Martha including her grand piano in the load. That grand piano was most important. It had a cut-out front lined with purple pleated silk and two lamps hung on bronze brackets. The lamps had pink silk shades, which were carefully packed among Martha's chemises and camisoles.

There was a fowl-coop tied beneath the dray and those fowls were expected to lay eggs every day, whatever the road was like. A cow was tied to the back of the dray to provide milk. She too was

4

expected to produce well, despite what the day had brought. Harris was not a man to tolerate non-productive animals.

Mt Cole is not famous for its rainfall in normal times, but for thirty-six hours before Harris's appointed time of departure the heavens wept. The bridge across the creek below the house disappeared beneath the yellow waters of the swollen stream. But Harris was a stubborn man. He left at the time he had originally decided. The bridge collapsed beneath the weight of the dray and the whole load sank slowly into the muddy water.

Harris roared and cursed, flogging the bullocks as they scrambled up the clay banks to draw the wagon from the flood. Martha shrieked and then wept as the purple pleated silk sank into the mud. History records neither what happened to the fowls and the cow nor what Martha said to her husband.

Great-grandmother Harris, as we knew her later, had plans for her five daughters to become 'real ladies' and the piano had a part in those plans. Sadly, it was never the same again.

In 1883 the only place in Melbourne where Harris could rest his bullocks was on the East Melbourne Common. He had planned to rest them for three days as he was anxious to move out to Officer but his wife, wanting the girls to see the big city, argued for a ten-day halt. She won.

During the ten days one bullock became ill. Harris's conviction that 'city kids' were useless became stronger when he mixed a drench and took it to the ailing bullock in a tin dipper. One of the children who had gathered to watch the team said, 'Look! He's going to give the cow a drink!' To Harris, any child who thought bullocks were cows and who thought that cows drank from tins was hardly worth raising.

Finally he manoeuvred Martha and the girls out of Melbourne and onto 260 hectares at Officer. The homestead was just a little to the east of the present pipeworks there. At this time, Lyall's homestead, 'Harewood', at Tooradin, was the social centre of the district. There were many balls conducted there and it was at these that his daughters were 'presented'. It took two days each way to cross the Koo Wee Rup Swamp to get to Tooradin, camping on the way. It must have been hard to look glamorous after camping out on the swamp all night!

The boys walked from Officer to Berwick to attend school, paying one shilling each per week for the privilege. They probably attended the school which used to stand on the corner of Manuka Road and the Gippsland Road, now the Princes Highway. There were two sons and they took turn and turn about, one going to school while the other minded the sheep, as there was neither time nor money for fencing. It says a great deal for their teachers and for home tutoring that both became well-educated men.

One son, William, farmed at Clyde and retired to live in Drouin. He had two children, Dick and Muriel, who both live in Drouin where Dick has a welding and engineering business. Muriel teaches at Neerim South High School. The other son, Walter, is farming at Yinnar. The long Harris connection with the land is continuing.

At Officer, Harris ran into financial trouble, so he took up a grazing lease near 'the island' to increase his carrying capacity. It was from this, a small area of higher ground, that Island Road was named. The land there provided a refuge for cattle during the frequent flooding of the swamp. Cattle were taken over in the spring as soon as a horseback reconnaissance showed that a buggy could get through to the lease, and were left there to fatten, being collected in the autumn. There were often considerable losses.

He also took work with Colonel Gipps at Berwick as a labourer. He bought a chaffcutter and hired it out in the summer. Eucalyptus distilling with the Tivendale family brought in a little more money but it was still a long time before the property began to pay its way. Before it did, Harris sold out. This was in 1888, after four years of great hardship. He bought a house in Bonney Street, Geelong, named after his sister's husband, but there was more money trouble. The man who bought the Officer property could not pay for it so Harris did not have the money due for the Geelong house. The family returned to Officer, eventually selling the place successfully and moving to Drouin.

Incidentally, the sister in Geelong, Mrs Bonney, lived to be one hundred and two years old. Among the presents she received on her one hundredth birthday, which fell on a Sunday, there came a load of firewood. Indignantly she ordered the carrier to remove it in case someone thought she had ordered wood on the Sabbath.

3 The Shy Old Master Craftsman from Drouin—Frank Tanner

Around Gippsland there are many people whose lives are the real material of the area's history. One such man is Frank Tanner, a cabinet-maker who has well earned the title of 'Master Craftsman'.

To Frank there is no such thing as a simple piece of wood. Each piece in the antique furniture he restores has a separate personality. Each requires special attention. The workmanship of 'F.E.T.', as he is known in the antiques trade, is the workmanship of an age gone by. His skills are skills that have been all but lost in the machine age. The pride he takes in his work and the care with which each piece is worked are the hallmarks of a man who learnt his trade in the days when perfection was the standard.

Frank was born in 1898 but wouldn't tell me where. He couldn't (or wouldn't) remember when he was married. He wouldn't let me take his photograph. His wife's full name and birthday were 'none of my business' (and they weren't, either).

As a young man he was persuaded by his father to become a clerk in Melbourne, but he wanted a trade. This was in the days when there were many Chinese cabinet-makers in Little Bourke Street. Young Frank spent his lunch hours watching them, and he still talks of the precision of their work. Eventually he gave up office work and began a five-year apprenticeship in cabinet making and joinery. His father must have changed his mind because he put up the £50 fee then necessary to obtain the training. He was paid three shillings per week at first, but by the end of his fifth year was earning £3, good money in those days.

The work of which he is most proud was the building of the Capitol Theatre, Melbourne, where 'there wasn't just any old wood used. It was all lined with Queensland silky oak. Every plank was checked over. It was a beautiful job.'

He spoke of working at Rawlinna, a sleeper depot on the Transcontinental Railway, out in the saltbush country 365 kilometres west of the South Australian border and 376 kilometres east of Kalgoorlie. On that job, 'F.E.T.' was part of a team which built twenty complete houses in just twenty-one days. The houses were not prefabricated but were completely assembled on site, the foundations being laid out with a huge wooden template and the walls covered with weatherboards and plywood lining before they were lifted into position. Those houses are still standing and are still quite sound.

One day at Rawlinna young 'F.E.T.' heard the warning cry 'Willy-willy!' The country was so flat that the willy-willies could be seen kilometres away but they moved with such great speed and changed direction so quickly that there was never any time to waste. He ran for shelter between two piles of sleepers.

The trouble came with the goat. There was a large herd at Rawlinna and they knew all about willy-willies from past experience. One particularly large and decidedly smelly billygoat dived behind the same pile of sleepers as 'F.E.T.'. It landed on top of him and refused to budge until the storm had passed!

Another amusing incident occurred during the building of the confessionals at the Roman Catholic Church in Colac. He and his mate were larking about as they finished the job. Wal, the off-sider, said that he would go around to the other side and hear Frank's 'confession'. Frank poured out a string of imaginary and hair-raising sins without realising that the parish priest, who had a memorable sense of humour, had persuaded Wal to wait outside while he heard the 'confession'.

After a time, Frank became a little uneasy at 'Wal's' replies. 'Is that you, Wal?' he asked. When a sombre voice answered, 'No, my son', the terrible truth dawned. 'F.E.T.' bolted out of the church and found Wal roaring with laughter. The priest thought it amusing, too.

We talked for a while about the Depression. The facts in the history books give no real idea of what this terrible period was really like. Frank was working on renovations at Maffra when the first blow fell. He drew his pay on the Friday, he remembers, but when he came to work on Monday he was told there was no more work and no more money.

With no work to be found the situation rapidly became desperate for the Tanners. Frank's mother came to stay with them and she mentioned that a shop was for sale in Warragul. The asking price was £100 and the Tanners were able to raise a total of £120. They went into business. The shop was rented and the £100 bought the goodwill and the stock. The stock consisted of one box of licorice straps, one 'silver stick' and two cases of apples on order.

Though times were hard, the Tanners gave good value and worked hard. They never became wealthy but they did get through the Depression better than many others. 'F.E.T.' remembers one touching story from those dark days. He was standing on the footpath when he saw a man moving slowly down the street, from time to time resting against the verandah poles. He had the usual bag on his shoulder and it was obvious that he was 'down on his luck'. When he reached 'F.E.T.' the following conversation took place.

'Good day.'

'Good day, mate. Hell! I know you from somewhere.'

'No', said Frank, 'there's no stone on my doorstep'. (A stone left on the doorstep by a wanderer was a sign that the people within would provide a meal for a man in need.)

They got talking about work, or the lack of it, and the Capitol Theatre came up in conversation. 'F.E.T.' thought that this was a ploy to gain an entrance so he tried a small trick.

'The Capitol Theatre job?' he asked. 'Wasn't very good wood they used on that, was it?' The wanderer replied with some heat that they had 'used the best damn silky oak in the country!'

'Who was your mate on the bench?' (The men had worked in pairs, one each side of the long workbenches.)

'I can't remember the name, but it was Turner, or Tanner, or something like that.'

Then Frank Tanner invited the man in. He had not recognised his old workmate. When the man left in the morning he was well fed and Frank had given him a blanket, an old pair of shoes and five shillings, all they could spare. Some six months later a letter came, saying that the writer now had a job and could repay the Tanners' kindness. Enclosed was a postal note for 7s 6d.

'Yes', said Frank, 'there were a lot of bludgers around in those days, but he was one of the genuine ones'.

Frank Tanner is now seventy-seven years old. He is still very much the master woodworker and still very hard at work. Frank Tanner wouldn't know what to do with himself if there wasn't a piece of cedar or mahogany about to be mended or stained or a chair needing repair. His hands need work to fill them.

4 Timberland!

Powelltown is a timber town. The forests of giant eucalypts which surround it provide the only reason for its existence and the mill and the Forests Commission are the only major employers in the area.

The upper regions of the Yarra Valley have long been a source of timber. In 1901 the largest mill in the whole region was Blake's Mill. This was to become Powelltown.

Blake built a tramway into the bush to bring the logs down to the mill but the sawn timber went to the railhead at Yarra Junction by road. The road was often impassable in winter so he began a tramway towards Yarra Junction. He made slow progress with this task and pressure from other users of the road, who objected to the damage done by the timber traffic, led to the formation of a public tramway company. This was the Gilderoy Tramway Company, which built ten kilometres of 91.4 cm gauge horse-drawn tramway. The maximum speed on the tramway was five kilometres per hour.

In 1912 the Powell wood preservation process was tried at Blake's Mill, as Powelltown was then still known. The mill was taken over by the Victorian Powell Wood Process Company in that year, but the experiment was not a success. Before the company failed, however, it had built a very good steel rail tramway to Yarra Junction. This tramway had official authority to carry passengers and it ran in competition with the Gilderoy Company's line.

The Powell Company was taken over by the Victorian Hardwood Milling and Seasoning Company. This company bought and closed the Gilderoy tramway in 1919. It also extended the tramway system into the Latrobe River watershed.

The ridge which divided the Little Yarra and Latrobe watersheds was known as 'The Bump'. In 1925 the company built a tunnel under The Bump, establishing a connection with the tramway system serving the Noojee areas. Other tramways radiated from the central line thus begun.

This was a period of expansion and unlimited confidence. The Warburton line was carrying the highest tonnage of any line in the state; Yarra Junction was the busiest station outside the metropolitan areas; there were four passenger stations between the Junction and Powelltown: Gladysdale, Black Sands, Three Bridges and Gilderoy. It seems incredible now that there should ever have been the population in the valley necessary for their function.

Powelltown was flourishing. It had a police station, a bank and several shops. There were twenty-nine houses and a huge boarding house in Yarra Street alone; now there are only seven or eight. The nearest police today are at Yarra Junction and the bank has been closed for thirty years.

The beginning of the decline of Powelltown came with the Depression of the 1930s. In 1928 there were 52,000 tonnes of timber sent through Yarra Junction, but by 1931 this annual tonnage had dropped to 12,000.

Fire has always been a great fear. The town is in an enclosed valley with vast stands of timber all around. It has been said that Powelltown has the best scenery in the state 'only yer can't see it fer the trees an' the hills!'

Fires in 1926 threatened to destroy the town. Considerable damage was done to the tramlines and bridges, but the great fires of 1939 were far more serious. They destroyed bridges, houses and mills out in the bush. Noojee was almost burnt out (as it had been in 1926) and it appeared that Powelltown was doomed.

These fires and the manpower shortages of the war put the company deeply in debt. In 1944 the demand for timber and a complete switch to road transport brought back the days of good profits but the town has never quite recovered the vitality it once enjoyed. Mechanisation has meant that fewer men were needed in the mill so it seems that Powelltown will never 'boom' again, although the mill, now owned by Australian Paper Manufacturers, is still a profitable concern.

Powelltown Primary School was, like the rest of the town, brought into being by the mill. A school was asked for on 25 April 1917, and was opened on 9 July of the same year. Things sometimes moved faster in those days than they do now! Until the school was opened local children walked to Gilderoy. The distance was not great (for those days) but the track was often impassable.

The mill provided the first school, a single eighteen metres by six metres building, rent free. It was opened under the first Headmaster, Francis L. Williamson. This room was also the local hall, which made it a very important community asset in the days when communities had to generate their own entertainment. It's dual purpose, unfortunately, led to problems and it was soon obvious that another building would be needed for the school.

The mill then offered to supply, completely free, all the timber for a new school. This was built near Blakes Creek, now a beautiful gully of treeferns. This larger school opened in June 1919. Another room was added in 1922, by which time the school had ninety pupils.

The residence was built in 1933 and the school was remodelled in 1938. At about this time two old railway carriages from Melbourne were being used as temporary classrooms; later they became shelter sheds but there is no trace of them today.

Strangely enough, there was another little primary school away in the hills to the east. It was called Powelltown Bush State School, perhaps one of the most appropriate names ever given a school. This school, serving the children of families attached to a small mill in the hills, was also known as Nayook West. Opened in October 1920, it was closed in 1939, during a decade in which the small mills disappeared and gave way to large, centralised operations.

Powelltown is still, above all else, a timber town. If you see it on a winter day when the clouds sit low on the hills and the colours are gone from the earth you will wonder how men could ever live there. If you feel that way, come back in the spring, when the colours return and the ranges roll away to the ends of the earth.

5 Phillip Island for Ten Pounds a Year!

Shipping today in Western Port Bay keeps well out from the large buoy that marks McHaffie's Reef. But in 1862 the only navigational aid in the bay was a small wooden beacon supporting a lamp on the high land behind the reef. That beacon was tended by Georgiana McHaffie, née Henderson.

From 1862 to 1883 Georgiana kept a diary which is still the best and most reliable source of information on the hard and bitter lives led by the first settlers of Phillip Island. It is a tale of hardship cheerfully endured, a tale of love and courage, a tale of endless effort on a new frontier.

William James McHaffie came to Australia aboard the *'Palmyra'*. His younger brother, James, died on the vessel on the voyage out, probably from typhoid fever. William then sent to Canada for his other brother, John David McHaffie.

William arrived in Melbourne on 23 November 1839, and the brothers established a station at Monnee Monnee Ponds, as it was then known. This was a temporary venture. By February 1843, the McHaffie brothers were preparing to move to Phillip Island. They had purchased a licence to occupy the whole of the island for £10 a year. If that seems rather generous, it should be remembered that the island was difficult to reach, had an uncertain water supply and was not considered to be very good land.

The brothers were the first real settlers on Phillip Island, though there were seven sealers living on the shore when they arrived. At first they had to negotiate the removal of a large herd of pigs belonging to Charles Manton, the 'Squire of Somerville', who had a station on the Mornington Peninsula. Most of the pigs were eventually removed but the survivors bred and, on occasion, provided a welcome change of diet for the McHaffies.

After five years the Government increased the annual licence fee to £17 10s. This was for a total of 9841 hectares. The land was cleared by the simple technique of burning it off and then picking up the remaining logs from any areas that needed to be ploughed. This was a standard technique in those days.

William apparently decided that Australia was not for him because he returned to Scotland, though he came back to Australia for a holiday later. John McHaffie stayed behind to run the station, and in March 1861, nearly twenty years after obtaining the island, he married Georgiana Jemima White Henderson, daughter of a Captain in the Royal Navy. She was a lady of considerable grace and ability who came to Victoria as a governess in 1852.

She was also the perfect settler's wife. A book on Phillip Island has said of her: 'She nursed her family and members of staff through various epidemics ... and also cared for cases of accident ... She was an efficient housekeeper, pianist and keen gardener ... baked bread for the station, made large quantities of jam, could set up a cask of home-made sherry, was a dressmaker ... and apparently thought nothing of riding for the mail to the Eastern Passage, twelve miles distant, shooting game, mustering sheep, or tending ewes during the lambing season.'

These are entries from her diary for 1862.

> Saturday *10* May. 'Left St Kilda for home. Reached the Long Beach restaurant at 9 o'clock.'
> Sunday *11* May. 'Slept on the table; went on in a dogcart; met Cavell who took us on to Snapper Point.'
> Monday *12* May. 'Left the "Mornington" for Sandy Point and reached the island just before dark.'

Snapper Point was an early name for what is now Mornington. Long Beach was probably an early name for Mordialloc.

The Acclimatisation Society used Phillip Island as something of a proving ground and McHaffie supported their activities. Deer were the most successfully experimented with and for a short time their numbers increased rapidly. In the 1860s he introduced three fallow deer, a buck and two roes. Red deer were also released. However, there were probably no deer left by 1920. They were believed to damage the chicory and potato crops so sportsmen from Melbourne joined local farmers in declaring war on the animals at an early date.

Strangely enough, there is very little recorded information about John D. McHaffie. It is known that he was a capable and diligent farmer. He saw the value of 'dipping' and had a sheep-dip built near the Newhaven Lagoon in 1867, forty-three years before dipping became compulsory. We know, too, that he struggled to prevent the island being thrown open for selection though he was of assistance to the selectors when they were finally allowed to take up parts of his run.

His foe in the battle to keep his station intact was Dr L. L. Smith, who represented the area in the Legislative Assembly from 1859 to 1894. Smith was a man of great eloquence and was tireless in his efforts to have the land open to all. Part of Smith's problem was that the government believed that the island was agriculturally worthless. In 1866 he succeeded in having a survey carried out. On 3 November 1868, there was at last a land sale on Phillip Island,

and on 26 December 1868 the township allotments at Rhyll were sold. Blocks at Cowes were offered for sale on 26 January 1869, with prices ranging from £8 to £41.

In 1868, with his holding on Phillip Island reduced to 202 hectares, McHaffie bought a property at Yanakie, on the isthmus of Wilsons Promontory. John Leeson went down to manage it in 1871 but the first load of wool was not brought up to Melbourne until 1873. The McHaffie diary has the entry: '*1873. January. Wednesday 1st*. Lock came from Yanakie with our first load of wool.'

One tale which has survived is of the day on which McHaffie decided to save some gunpowder which had become wet in a boating accident. He dried the gunpowder in a fry-pan over an open fire, bending over to stir it with a spoon so that it should dry evenly! Apparently the rest of the household found work that required attending to elsewhere until the perilous task was finished. Perhaps it is true after all that the one thing a Scot cannot face is waste!

6 The Gippsland Fleet and the Men Who Sailed It

Ships and the men who sailed them on our coasts and inland waterways played a vital and colourful role in our history. There are now only a few fading signs of the busy shipping industry which once served the Gippsland Lakes and the eastern coast of Victoria, but the stories still remain.

Along the lakes and rivers the old wharves are slowly rotting away. Each flood carries away a few more timbers, a few more planks. The old boats are nearly all gone. Some were lost at sea. Some were burnt at their moorings. Many were laid up in some quiet backwater to slowly rot and then slide beneath the muddy waters of a winter flood.

The fishing boats still go out over the Lakes Entrance bar and the fibreglass catamarans chase abalone outside Mallacoota and Gabo but the old romance is gone. Gone, too, are the old sailors who built their own boats and carried no compass, no charts and no radio.

On 2 January 1841, the paddle steamer *Clonmel* went aground on the bar that bears its name in Corner Inlet. All aboard survived and they reported good farming land near where the ship grounded. In the previous year, Count Paul Strzelecki had passed through the same area and these two factors led directly to the growth of a settlement at Port Albert.

This port was used to ship cattle from Gippsland to Tasmania. The goldrushes in the Gippsland hills provided more traffic and during the 1850s Port Albert became a busy little area.

John Reeve came to Port Albert in July 1842. In the same year he explored the coast to the east and was probably the second white man to see what is now Lakes Entrance. Lake Reeve is named after him. Sixteen years later, in 1858, a bold young Scot named Malcolm Campbell sailed the *Georgina Smith* through the entrance, down Lake Bunga and up the Tambo River toward Bruthen. This bold feat captured the attention of many a Melbourne investor.

Campbell came to Gippsland as a government surveyor in 1846. Later he purchased a property with a lake frontage. He had always been a keen yachtsman and he soon built up a detailed knowledge of local waters. The *Georgina Smith* was a wooden schooner of eighteen metres. Campbell used her as a trader on the Gippsland coast until 1865, when she was sold to a Warrnambool dweller.

Before Campbell crossed the bar for the first time there were already boats trading on the Lakes. They were unable, however, to ship produce anywhere outside the immediate area. This was in the days before the Gippsland Railway was built. The track that was to become the Princes Highway was still only a pack track and was often impassable. It is easy, therefore, to assess the importance of Campbell's feat.

A Mr McArdel of Sale constructed a steamer, the *Enterprise*, at Sale Common in 1858. A convenient flood carried her across to the Latrobe River and she was launched at the Longford wharf. This vessel traded up and down the lakes for many years but her owner didn't get around to having her registered until 1863.

In 1864 the Gippsland Lakes Navigation Company began a steamship service between Melbourne and the Gippsland Lakes. Initially they relied on the thirty-nine-metre steamer *Charles Edward*, powered by a single sixty horsepower engine. It was often necessary for a small dinghy to precede her through the entrance to search out the shifting channel. The same company ran the steamer *Samson* based at Port Albert.

In 1866 a group of Melbourne businessmen placed the *Trio* on the run to the Lakes. She was a paddle steamer with schooner rigging 'just in case'. After one year she ran aground on the entrance. While she was aground the entrance shifted, leaving her a long way from the water!

Other well-known boats on the Lakes in the 1860s were the *Thomas Norton*, a converted Melbourne tugboat, *The Lady Of The Lakes* and the *Lady Darling*, which was built on the Tambo River.

Navigation around the coast was a highly dangerous pastime in those years. Ships frequently 'bumped' while crossing the bar at what is now known as Lakes Entrance, once called Cunninghame. There was very little shelter outside in the Strait. Gabo Island and Wilsons Promontory offered the only safe anchorages and these were several hours away.

In 1882 the skipper of the *Pretty Jane* ran her aground to save the crew, as she could make no headway in the storm that was raging. The same storm drove the schooner *Glengarry* ashore on the 'ninety-mile' beach. The *Magnolia*, another schooner, was driven ashore near Lake Tyers and the *Gippslander* was wrecked at Gabo Island.

Even in good weather, navigation was difficult. Charts were often wildly inaccurate and much of the coastline was relatively featureless. There were no lighthouses until 1859 when the Cape Schank and South-East Point (Wilsons Promontory) lights were built. Fog was a common hazard. Three years later the Gabo Island light was built in 1862. Another twenty-two years were to pass before the Cliffy Island light was erected in 1884. Cape Everard, now re-named Point Hicks, had a lighthouse in 1890 and another was erected at Cape Liptrap in 1913. Thus, in the 1860s there were only three lights between Port Phillip and the New South Wales border.

One very famous vessel on the lakes was the *Tanjil*, a paddle steamer twenty-four metres long built on the Yarra in 1877. She was powered by a single-cylinder engine with a 91.4cm stroke and a 40.6 cm bore! She traded between Sale and Bairnsdale and was tied up at the Bairnsdale wharf on 29 January 1885, when she caught fire. She was cut free to save the wharf and shedding and the fire died only when her hull finally settled beneath the water.

Another vessel which achieved even greater fame was the steamer *Gippsland*, built by J.C. Dahlsen. Launched in 1908, she was the largest vessel ever built in Gippsland. Always a popular boat on the Lakes, she was taken over by the Royal Australian Navy in World War II and became *H.M.A.S. Gippsland*. She was lost in a storm off the New Hebrides.

An amusing tale illustrates the nature of the men who sailed this midget fleet. The *Advance* was nearing the Mallacoota Bar in rough weather when the skipper saw three large waves bearing down upon him. He tried to bring the ship's bows around to meet the waves but was too late. The first wave swamped her and stopped her dead in the water. The second wave rolled her over, but the third returned her to an upright position and the skipper continued the voyage without a pause. The engines never even stopped!

7   There's Gold in Gippsland's Hills!

Look north to the rugged slopes of the Great Dividing Range from almost anywhere in Gippsland and the chances are that you are looking at an old goldfield.

The main fields for the big companies were at Walhalla, Dargo, Bullumwaal (near Bairnsdale), Cassilis (near Omeo) and Bendoc, which isn't near anywhere. The three main West Gippsland fields were at Warragul, Noojee and Warrandyte. Warrandyte is not really in West Gippsland but it is on the mountain feature which relates most closely to that area.

Victoria's Legislative Council appointed a Select Committee to administer the claims for rewards for gold discoveries. On 10 March 1854, this committee reported that it had paid the sum of £1,000 to L. J. Michel and party, in recognition of their discovery of gold at Andersons Creek, near Warrandyte.

Louis John Michel was an Englishman who came to Australia before the gold rushes. When rewards were offered for discoverers of the precious metal he formed a prospecting party, which began its search on the property of a Major Newman, late of the 51st Bengal Native Infantry. On retiring to Australia, Newman had bought a farm on the Yarra River. The prospectors found quartz and then alluvial gold. The first discoveries were made about a kilometre east of the bridge at the southern end of the present township.

Great hopes were held by the miners and there was a rush to the area. The field was never very profitable and, though mining continued for some years, yields were always small.

A month after Michel's Warrandyte discovery there was a major find at Buninyong and most of the miners joined the new rush. Now the alluvial deposits in Andersons Creek and the Yarra are worked only by 'weekend' prospectors, who sometimes recover small quantities of gold. The people of Warrandyte still dispute with the people of Clunes over which was the first goldfield to be opened-up in Victoria. The debate is an academic one because the Warrandyte fields never were very significant.

It is not generally known that Warragul was a 'gold station' for some years but the surprising truth is that there is a large area of gold-bearing country around Warragul and a number of mines have been operated in the district. Early in the 1860s James Vesey and Peter Matassi began mining at Crossover, once called Flume, north of Warragul. They followed a number of 'tin dish' prospectors who were working the creeks running down from the nearby ranges. The opening of their mine halted the building of the telegraph line to Warragul, for all the linesmen rushed to seek work at the new mine.

Vesey and Matassi called their mine the 'Happy Go Lucky' but the name was over-optimistic. The gold was patchy and the miners were soon in financial strife. Henry Lancaster opened a mine next to the 'Happy Go Lucky' and soon he, too, went 'broke'.

Milners had operated a mine at Walhalla. They came to Crossover and re-opened the 'Happy Go Lucky', but they had no better luck than the previous operators. A syndicate of Warragul businessmen then bought the mine and renamed it, aptly enough, the 'Perseverance'. Again it slowly petered out.

Prospectors Creek, south of Warragul, was named after Joe Martin, who worked the small creeks along the north side of the Strzelecki Ranges. In 1857 gold was discovered in Heifer Creek at Ripplebrook. Another creek nearby was named Gold Creek and there was gold in Bear Creek also, to which there was a small rush in1882. All these creeks are south of Drouin.

A 'Mr Champion' operated the most successful 'mine' in the region and added a little colour to the history of such enterprises. He opened a mine south of Warragul and installed a very impressive array of machines to work it. He sold shares in this new venture and, when all the shares were sold, left the district with the cash! At least there was one man who made a good profit out of the Warragul goldfield.

The creeks in the hills around Noojee have long been an attraction for prospectors, some of whom have been very successful. Far and away the best-known of these mountain men was old Dick Belpoole. Dick was an eccentric old Englishman who poked about in the rugged country north of Noojee for many years. He only came out of the scrub to buy supplies — and to sell his gold. When the scrub proved too much for his store-bought clothes, old Dick made himself a suit of tin. It lasted well, though it can't have been any too comfortable. The look of it didn't matter. Dick regarded the rest of the human race as something of nuisance.

Naturally, the people of Noojee came to regard this bearded hillbilly with a good deal of interest. After all, whenever he entered the town he was carrying gold, and often in large quantities. Some tried to follow him back into the bush but he always eluded them. Others tried to loosen his tongue by buying him drinks, but all he ever told them was that he had discovered the 'mother lode'. No-one ever found his mine.

Eventually, old Dick was removed to an old people's home in Melbourne 'for his own good'. One young adventurer rescued Dick from the home on condition that Dick would lead him to the lode. They set off into the bush but Dick died before he showed the location of the gold. Perhaps there is still a fortune to be made in those hills but, wherever Dick Belpoole is now, his secret is still safe.

In the narrow, cramped little valley of Stringers Creek and the Walhalla township there are still the workings of the Long Tunnel, the Long Tunnel Extended, and the other mines that once filled the valley with the roar of crushers.

The Long Tunnel mine achieved fame as the richest gold mine in Victoria at a time when the Ballarat and Bendigo fields were in full production. The Long Tunnel yielded 815,568 tray ounces of gold and paid dividends totalling more than £1,250,000. That gold had come from a long way down. The mine had an inclined shaft of 1234 metres and then a vertical shaft of another 183 metres. It was one of the deepest mines in the world.

Stockyard Creek saw a minor goldrush in October 1870, and two years later gold was discovered in nearly Turtons Creek. Both of these finds were near Foster, but they never amounted to much. Gold was also found on the Baw Baw Plateau as early as January 1860; there were also several significant finds at Tanjil. The Woods Point field was discovered in January, 1865, and soon became very important.

These finds and fields did much more than make and break personal fortunes. The movement of diggers into Gippsland added to the demand for roads and places of shelter and refreshment, and many became farmers and storekeepers. Much of the development of the province was accelerated greatly by the gold finds.

8 Angus McMillan—Port Albert's Unsung Hero

Angus McMillan did not mind hard work if there was a dollar (or a sovereign) to be made by it. Few of our explorers were entirely altruistic in their motivation. The unsung hero of the opening-up of central Gippsland had one main object in mind: he wanted to raise fat cattle for the market in Van Diemens Land, and that meant finding grazing land and a port somewhere on the southern coastline.

The first white people to see the area that became Port Albert were the survivors of the stranding of the 524-tonne barque *Clonmel*. Her captain, Mr Tulleroy, discovered the port by the simple but rather dramatic method of becoming lost and running aground in it.

The ship grounded on Snake Island on the morning of 2 January 1841. It was not badly damaged and no lives were lost. A passenger named Simpson admitted to some sailing experience and was sent off in a boat with a crew of five to seek help. They were found by a boat from Tasmania which took them to Williamstown, where they arrived only sixty-three hours after the *Clonmel* went aground.

Meanwhile, Angus McMillan was exploring in Gippsland. He had not yet reached the coast of South Gippsland.

Top: The cover of the menu for the dinner celebrating the opening of the Gippsland Railway (see Story 1). Bottom left: William Harris, Junior, and his wife, Ethel (see Story 2). Bottom right: Frank Tanner in his workshop (see Story 3)

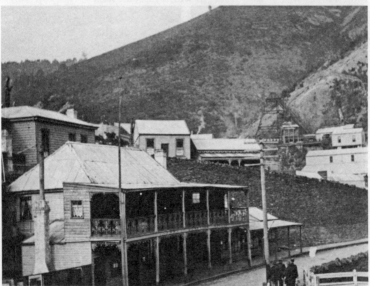

*Top: The aftermath of a fire at Powelltown Mill on 2 May 1976:
the town's future in doubt—again (see Story 4). Photo: Age Suburban Publications.
Bottom: Walhalla around 1910 (see Story 7). Photo: Country Roads Board, Victoria*

The survivors of the *Clonmel* were taken to Melbourne by two cutters sent from Williamstown to rescue them, the *Will Watch* and *The Sisters*. The ninety passengers, the crew and the mail were all picked up safely at their makeshift camp on Snake Island. (Both Snake Island and Clonmel Island still appear on maps of the area.) A Mr Grose of Sydney bought the wreck for £110, using the schooner *Eliza* to ferry salvage back to Sydney.

The wrecked passengers had found a good channel into Corner Inlet and their report, and the interest created by Count Paul Strzelecki, led to the formation of the Gippsland Company. The good gentlemen of this company, Messrs Hawdon, Orr, Rankin, Brodribb, McLeod, Kirsopp and Stewart, chartered the 300-tonne *Singapore* (after which Mt Singapore on Wilsons Promontory was named) for their survey.

The *Singapore* reached Snake Island on 13 February 1841, but it took some days to locate the channel into the inlet. Two of the wrecked *Clonmel* boats were found and acted as a landmark. When the channel was found, it led to well-grassed grazing country.

The port was promptly named Port Albert and the men built a small cottage. They did not know that while they were searching for the channel Angus McMillan had come to the very spot where they landed and then gone on again. McMillan was partly driven by a fierce desire to prove that those who believed that there was no southern port on the coast were wrong. When he reached Port Albert there was a depth of two metres even at low tide, where today there is little more than mud.

McMillan went back to report to his employer and partner, Macalister, but Governor Latrobe made a grant of the area to the Gippsland Company, soon to be renamed the Port Albert Company. Governor Gipps later revoked the grants and the security of the young settlement was threatened.

Further east, near what is now Yarram, another strange settlement was growing. Aeneas Ronaldson MacDonell, chief of the Glengarry sept of the MacDonell Clan, had arrived there with a 'court' of Scots. He lived in feudal splendour for a year but the venture was a financial disaster. He sold out, disbanded his followers and returned to Sydney. He died in New Zealand, half a world away from the graves of his ancestors.

Meanwhile, McMillan persisted in his efforts to develop a cattle trade through Port Albert. The *Port Phillip Patriot* of 29 August 1842, reported a Tasmanian newspaper as saying: 'The "*Waterwitch*" has brought a cargo of fat cattle which met with a ready sale. We went to look at a pair of the fattest bullocks we have ever seen in the colony, which were brought over by McMillan as a specimen of 500 more he has ready for shipment at Port Albert.' This was only eighteen months after the port was discovered. During 1842 McMillan shipped more than 900 head of cattle on the *Waterwitch* and the *Agenoria*. At least three other vessels were also used.

By the end of 1842 the settlement had a population of about 220, including thirty-three bond and twenty-six free women. Many of these people lived in huts along the beach waiting for the town allotments to be surveyed and put up for sale. A number of escapees from Van Diemens Land came across the Strait in stolen boats and as stowaways, several of them to become minor bushrangers in the area. There was also a strong trade in smuggled spirits and tobacco. Law and order appeared with the appointment of Charles James Tyers as Crown Lands Commissioner, who arrived in Port Albert on 13 January 1844.

Tyers made several attempts to come overland with a police escort and all due pomp and ceremony, but finally he had to come by ship with very little fuss. Like many petty officials, Tyers was a hard man to like. One resented act was to declare war on the beachfront settlers who had erected 'unlicenced huts' and on other petty offenders.

The locals had by now discovered that a ship could come in quite close to Shipping Point, on the west side of the Tarra River, and much stock was transferred to the ships there by punt, thus evading more licence fees.

In 1844 Governor Latrobe came to Port Albert and, impressed by the development taking place, he approved the setting up of a Court of Petty Sessions. Agitation for a road to Melbourne was heard, but that achievement was still a long way off. Port Albert was now 'on the map' but Angus McMillan received no reward or recognition for his exploration of that portion of Gippsland. Yet the Polish Count Paul Edmund de Strzelecki was feted and admired as the hero of Gippsland exploration.

McMillan set up a homestead at Bushy Park, the house now being in the Moe Folk Museum and containing a number of items related to McMillan and the period. He became known as a convivial host, and one of his frequent guests was Dr Alexander Arbuckle, an interesting and colourful character.

Arbuckle was practising medicine at Omeo when, on one occasion, he was required to attend court in Melbourne to give evidence in a murder trial. He was so offended at the interruption to his practice and the hardship of his journey that he promptly wrote to the Port Phillip Gazette and announced that the Medical Board of New South Wales could remove his name from their register. Eventually he resumed his practice and became a popular doctor in a number of South Gippsland communities in later years.

McMillan was appointed Protector of Aborigines and Bushy Park became a popular camp site for many of them. He also kept a room at the Port Phillip Club Hotel for the use of newly-arrived Scots until they were able to find their own quarters, and he became a leading member of the Gippsland Caledonian Society.

In 1858 this grand old Gippslander became the first member for South Gippsland in the Legislative Assembly. Finding that politics was not to his liking, he withdrew in November 1860. He died in May 1865, after a packhorse slipped and fell on him at Iguana Creek. At the time of his death he was trying to cut a track for which he had a government contract. It was typical of the man that he continued almost singlehanded when his men left him to search for gold. He was on his way to recruit more men when he lost his life.

9 James Pennycuick— Long-distance Farmer

Whether it was from a hunger for land or a sense of adventure, the vast majority of those who took up land in Gippsland bore names like Macalister, McMillan, McArdle, Stewart and Ross. In the town of Budgeree, one of the first settlers was James Pennycuick, of Motherwell, near Glasgow, Scotland.

Somehow the history books have overlooked Pennycuick and most of our knowledge of him comes from a document he wrote in

July 1932. The purpose of the document is not clear and the writing is difficult to read, but the story it tells is a fascinating one, offering a glimpse of the lengths to which our ancestors would go to establish themselves on land they could call their own.

James married Maggie Burnside, of Overtown, Scotland, on 4 June 1878, and spent the next five years running a business which belonged to his mother-in-law. His brother-in-law, Michael Burnside, was in poor health and it was decided that the climate of New Zealand might benefit him. James Pennycuick, now twenty-seven years old, accompanied Michael and his uncle, one Robert Millar. They took a train to Tilbury docks and there boarded the steamship *Iberia*. Mrs Pennycuick and her family were left behind to 'mind the store'.

The travellers made their first Australian landfall at Albany, Western Australia, and then came on to Adelaide and Melbourne. The S. S. *Manapouri* took them across the Tasman to New Zealand. In that country they searched for a suitable property, finally buying a farm at Bluenose, about sixteen kilometres from Dunedin. Pennycuick stayed there a few weeks but as soon as Millar and Burnside were settled in he took the steamer *Ringarooma* to Lyttelton from Port Chalmers. The *Doric* took him back to London via Cape Horn and Rio de Janeiro. His Maggie met him at Law Junction and drove him home to Overtown, from which he had been away for nearly six months.

A few weeks later his mother-in-law decided to join her son in New Zealand so James escorted her to London, but she sailed without any company in the *British Queen*. James went back to Overtown and spent the next two years there with Maggie, running the business for Mrs Burnside and also working for Thomas Barr, a commercial traveller. Eventually, and probably inevitably, they decided to migrate to Australia, so Pennycuick sailed from Greenock with his wife, his son Thomas, his daughters Isabella and Janet, his brother Thomas and William Millar. They went via the Cape of Good Hope to Albany and then Hobart, and from Tasmania they sailed to New Zealand and the farm at Bluenose.

James and Thomas Pennycuick, and Robert Millar, then sailed back to Melbourne via Hobart (the Pennycuicks never took short cuts!) and met 'Uncle Burnside'. Their search for work at Frankston was without success; then James found a job with John Duncan at Neerim. When the Neerim job ended Pennycuick, Millar and

Burnside went to the Land Board at Traralgon, for land at Budgeree had been recommended to them. Millar and Pennycuick went on to Yinnar where they leased a paddock from W. H. Wicks living in a hut belonging to him. This paddock, they improved, then exchanging it for one behind the Yinnar Railway Station.

At this point Pennycuick returned to New Zealand to collect Maggie and the children, this being a common procedure. Many settlers left their families behind while they came out here and established a property and a home; then they sent for the women and children when the wilderness was sufficiently tamed. It must have been a lonely business for all concerned.

In 1886 he bought two blocks of land from Hicks and built a house for his family, shortly after this buying a farm across the Morwell River and renting the Yinnar house to one Thomas Walsh. The Burnsides still in New Zealand then came to Australia to join Pennycuick at Budgeree.

During the period in which he was establishing the farm at Budgeree, Pennycuick lived in Yinnar and travelled across the river whenever he had the time to spare. At about this time he was appointed manager of the butter factory, of which he was also a director, for two years. When he resigned the other directors gave him a present of £20 and a framed testimonial.

He tried without success to sell the Budgeree farm but then placed it under the management of Archibald Burnside, Maggie's brother, and Mrs Burnside, senior, who both lived on it. His family had grown in the meantime. 'Maggie, Willie and Minnie' now make their first appearance in his record. In 1893 the whole family boarded the *Oceania* in Melbourne and returned to Motherwell; only six or seven months later he was headed back to Melbourne in the *Oruba*. This was in 1894.

He returned to Yinnar and took over the Yinnar store from Thomas Walsh. This was his business for eleven years until he moved onto another farm at Budgeree, one of sixty-five hectares. He was to stay on this farm for twenty-five years. It was from here that his son, Willie, left to go to war. He never returned, having been killed at Pozieres in 1916.

Before he moved back on to the farm, in about 1906, Pennycuick again became a director of the butter factory. He was also secretary of it for three years and finally the liquidator when the factory was sold to Wood and Company of Melbourne. These appointments alone make it seem strange that his name is barely known in the area.

In one way and another, he owned a good deal of land in the township area at various times. He sold the house in Yinnar to a Mrs Donaldson of Morwell, a township block to Thomas Walsh, two blocks near the hotel and the store to John Moore, the original farm to Thomas Walsh and two blocks known as 'Deppeler's' and 'Yinnar' to the Closer Settlement Board. He also handed over 'Kelvin Grove', the farm he bought in 1906, to his son, James. Finally, he and his wife went to live at 'Bannockburn', the home of one of his daughters who had married R. J. Elliott.

Maggie Pennycuick died at 'Bannockburn' on 10 October 1931, and the document written by her husband closes with the rather sad lines: 'I am still living here alone on the 30th July, 1932. I still retain the 277 hectares of freehold land at Budgeree which I selected over 46 years ago.'

We know very little of James Pennycuick beyond what is in that document. We do know that he made a successful application in 1905 for a school at Budgeree in a room of his house. (This date, incidentally, indicates that he may have purchased the second farm at Budgeree in 1905 rather than 1906.) In August 1908, the Education Department leased another, larger building from him. This was destroyed by fire in December of the same year but Pennycuick rebuilt it and the school reopened in March 1909. This was school No. 3504, Budgeree South East, which finally closed in 1954.

There is little else to be said about Pennycuick, simply because little else seems to be known. We might well wonder why a man of such apparent ability and endeavour, and who played such a significant part in the growth of the district, should be nearly forgotten.

10 Warragul? Not Worth 45 Pence!

Try to imagine it — a vast silent area of towering forest, broken only by a narrow track winding to the east. That was Warragul 105 years ago. Lyrebirds were common in the deep gullies and the swamps to the south. Cobb and Co had a stables at Brandy Creek, to the north.

The Warragul area was part of the Tarween Run, owned by Thomas Walton of Berwick. Walton had bought the rights to the area between the Bunyip River and Whisky Creek for £45. He did this to secure first choice of the 259-hectare lots into which the area was being divided, but his comment was that the whole run 'was not worth forty-five pence'.

Following the 1869 Land Act, James Young settled at Drouin West in May of that year. He was followed by James Hann at Brandy Creek, and John Rogers came from Churchill Island, in Western Port, to take up land beside Hann. Hann and Young tried the simple process of burning-off the scrub and scattering grass seed in the ashes, which was instantly successful. It could be argued that this experiment marked the beginning of Warragul's long march to the prosperity it enjoys today.

One colourful early resident was Solomon Kinsey, who lived in a hollow log near the original track. He sold his land (and log) and took up residence in another log near the Brandy Creek post office. He found his new home quite unsuitable. Being so close to the road, he was pestered by swagmen who had been kicked out of the new hotel and were looking for somewhere to spend the night!

At this time the scrub was so dense that James Hann was able to make a good living guiding selectors to their properties. He had an Aboriginal with him, called Toby, whose sense of direction served better than a compass when it was time to return to their hut.

Another early settler achieved distinction by having a name that has since become a term of abuse. This was Moses Fink.

The flat country south of Warragul was regarded by most as a useless and impenetrable swamp, but gradually it was settled and it was always 'the next few miles' that were useless. South of Darnum and Nilma the land was also regarded as being too swampy to be of any use. But slowly the settlers made headway. The giant trees of the forest all but disappeared and good green pasture spread over the rich, red volcanic soil.

No talk of the early years of Warragul should neglect James Lardner. Lardners Track is a reminder of the men most often forgotten in local history, the surveyors. James Lardner was ordered to survey a line due south from the Coach Road at Brandy Creek to the projected line of the Great Southern Railway. His survey came out within centimetres of the intended point, though for sixteen kilometres he had been forced to cut a track just to obtain room to use his theodolite. Lardner also surveyed and laid out the other towns around Warragul and later the settlements along the railway into South Gippsland.

The first Court of Petty Sessions opened in Warragul in November, 1878. The first County Court in Warragul sat in 1880 and by this time Warragul had a constable. Respectability was fast approaching.

The Gippsland Railway was opened in 1878 and this caused an immediate 'boom' in the commercial growth of Warragul. The importance of the railway can be understood when it is realised that one and a half kilometres an hour was considered fast walking in that country at the time and a horse could carry only forty-five kilograms.

Of course, men could work up a thirst in that kind of country and hotels played a major part in the early development of the township. One hotel was operating at Shady Creek by 1872. The first hotel in the township itself was probably the Royal Hotel, opened by Elizabeth Hagin in 1878. The unlicenced Crown Hotel was originally on Crown land but eventually was moved to the site of the Orient Hotel. The Railway Hotel was opened by George Streitberg in 1879; then came the Commercial and Club Hotels. It was also in the 1870s that the enterprising Henry Dicken built the Robin Hood Hotel, a well-known landmark now operating as a motel. Dicken also built a brewery and a cordial factory near his hotel.

The area was well-supplied with racehorses, a racehorse in those days being any horse that could run faster than any other horse. Races were conducted outside the Turf Club Hotel and there are still some wonderful tales told about bolters. A racecourse was opened at Whisky Creek and the course is still in use — but that is another story.

In 1894 the Warragul Racing Club was formed but there was a little trouble with the course. One squatter refused to move and had to be bought out at the great cost of £6. On Boxing Day 1895, the first Warragul Cup was run as part of a very successful meeting. The track is now Logan Park and, though the Warragul Racing Club has faded from the scene, some very good horses in a different harness are still to be seen racing there.

Warragul was at first part of the Buln Buln Shire, gazetted in 1878. Only three years later, the Shire of Warragul was created by severance from the Buln Buln Shire, officially on 9 December 1881. The new Shire held its first meeting on 15 February 1882. A secretary was appointed for four weeks at £2 per week and applications were called for the combined positions of secretary, engineer, rate collector and dog-tax collector!

A rate of one shilling in the pound was struck and the rate collector reported having collected £44. 16s. There was some dismay among residents at the rate imposed, which became greater when it was proposed that a 'tram rate' of 2s 6d in the pound be charged to finance the construction of a tramway to the south of the town.

In 1892 the railway line to Neerim was begun. This line eventually extended to Noojee, while there were unsuccessful attempts to promote support for other lines from Warragul to Leongatha and to Mirboo. For a time Warragul was seen as a potentially major rail junction.

These brief notes do little justice to the colourful history of Warragul. Perhaps more justice was done with the award of the 'Premier Town' title in 1970.

11 The Great Southern Railway Epic

In the 1870s there was a land rush in South Gippsland, which was brought about by the 1869 Land Act and the thousands of men searching for farming land after the gold rushes of the 1860s.

Access was the problem in South Gippsland, cut off from Melbourne by the almost-impenetrable Koo Wee Rup Swamp. By 1877, newspapers from Melbourne could reach Sale on the day they were printed but the same newspapers took four days to reach Foster. Selectors needing equipment or stores, or wishing to send produce to Melbourne from the far south, had a limited choice. They could depend on the small coastal vessels or they could use the coach to Sale and the railway from there to Melbourne. Further north, the settlers at Poowong could send goods to the railway station at Drouin. In all cases, the service was slow and uncertain.

Soon, the dissatisfied settlers began to agitate for a railway into South Gippsland, forming 'Railway Leagues' to organise the campaign. Though these often claimed to have more members than there were people living in the area, and though their suggestions were often wildly impracticable, they were eventually successful. In 1887 the Great Southern Railway was begun. The first section was from Dandenong to Whitelaws Track (Korumburra) and took five years to complete. Falkingham and Sons, the contractors, who had built the Caulfield to Frankston line, tendered a price of almost £3,500 per mile.

The second section of track ran from Whitelaws Track to Toora. The contract for this was let to Andrew O'Keefe at a price of £322,693 17s 11d, about £3,000 per mile. The last major section, from Toora to Palmerston (Port Albert), was let to Buckley and Sons, contractors who had built several lines in the Western District. The contract price was £72,072 17s 10d, about £3,000 per mile. All three sections were completed by the end of 1891 and the first train ran through from Melbourne to Port Albert on 13 January 1892.

The problems the contractors faced and surmounted were incredible. Falkingham had to cross the Koo Wee Rup Swamp. To do this, he built four separate bridges in every one and a half kilometres of track to allow for the drainage of floodwaters. Each bridge was ninety-one metres long. The bridge-over the 'Main Drain' had 137 openings for the water to pass through, each of them over three metres wide. Dalmore Station, originally named Peers Lane, was in such a wet location that the platform was built on piles and a rowboat was kept at the station for the use of passengers!

Falkingham doubted that it would ever be possible to drain the swamp but he reported that the soil seemed very fertile and would be of great value if it could be drained. The land was so wet that the twenty-three kilometres of steep hills and swampy gullies between Bena and Leongatha took two years to survey, though there were twelve men working on the task.

O'Keefe ran into problems that were even worse than those facing Falkingham. To cross the Tarwin River he had to built three trestle bridges, two of 152 metres and one of 305 metres in length. Between Korumburra and Toora he had to make countless cuttings and the work on these was often interrupted by landslides. At Black Spur, near Tarwin, 23,000 cubic metres had to be moved out of one cutting after a landslide.

There was no real road to bring in supplies so everyone used the railway clearing as a roadway. Even Cobb and Co sometimes ran coaches down the clearing. Feed for the horses and bullocks was also a problem. There was no grass in the dense forests so all feed had to be transported. Horses and bullocks were used in great numbers, and the problem of transporting sufficient food for them was made much worse by the fact that it was a ten-day trip to the end of the line and in that time the packhorses usually ate about a third of their load and needed some for the return trip as well.

The forests were dense and some of the trees were huge. They were, fortunately, suitable for sleeper-cutting but, even so, the cost of clearing usually worked out in the vicinity of £2,000 per mile in this section. O'Keefe also had to build a wharf and five kilometres of track at Port Franklin, at his own expense, to bring in his equipment.

Buckley had by far the best section, from Toora to Alberton, but even he had problems. He was unable to land his locomotive at the wharf in Toora as he had planned, so he built a staging in open water at the side of the channel! Imagine the problems of building a staging, or landing, in the shifting mud of Corner Inlet and then transferring a locomotive onto it from the decks of a tiny schooner. These were resourceful men.

There were many accidents and some were serious. Two men were blown apart at Hoddle. Buckley's locomotive, the *Ivanhoe*, ran over a cow and fell upside-down into a swamp. It took weeks to bring it back into service. On a high bridge over the Tarwin River O'Keefe's locomotive ran into a mob of bullocks. The bridge was so high that the natives riding the open wagons could not jump to safety. By some miracle the locomotive and train stayed upright on the bridge, though it was off the rails.

At Kardella a group of ballast trucks was involved in what could very easily have become a major tragedy. It was the practice to let the trucks run downhill from Korumburra to Ruby with no engine, letting gravity do the work. With fourteen people riding on the trucks, one of these 'gravity trains' collided head-on with the contractor's locomotive. The impact destroyed the engine and yet no-one was badly hurt!

Many of the place names of those days have now disappeared. Peers Lane became Koo Wee Rup West and then Dalmore.

Glasscocks became Monomeith. Koo Wee Rup was originally Yallock. Lang Lang was named Carrington and then Tobin Yallock. The Brickyards is now Kardella. Cummings became Coalition Creek and then Ruby. Foster was once known as Stockyard Creek.

Not only the names have changed. The towns themselves have altered with the years. For most, the railway brought rapid growth. Timber, coal, fish, cattle, dairy produce, vegetables and even tin from the Toora mines could now be sent swiftly and cheaply to the markets in Melbourne.

There was a subdivisional sale in Koo Wee Rup in March 1890. Korumburra was surveyed in 1887 and lots were sold by public auction in 1888. These dates reflected the coming of the railway. Lines were extended to Coal Creek in 1892, Jumbunna in 1894, Outtrim in 1896, Woolamai in 1910, Strzelecki in 1922, Yarram in 1922 and Woodside in 1923, each addition bringing the communities of South Gippsland a little closer to Melbourne. One grisly note is that the line at Toora was laid across the town's small cemetery and one body, it is said, still lies beneath the permanent way.

12 The Restoration of a Saintly Lady

'St Germaine' was one of five big properties that spread across the western part of the Koo Wee Rup Swamp before the rush of selectors in the 1870s. Only 202 hectares now, the title once covered 2,428 of the best hectares on the swamp.

Yvonne and Allan Knowles, the present owners of the historic 'St Germaine' homestead, are spending much time and effort on bringing their home back to its former beauty. Their task is a huge one, for the building is of double-brick construction and parts of it have been allowed to fall into disrepair.

It was originally owned by Alexander Patterson, who had come to Port Phillip in 1841. Seven years later he moved to the area on the Karr Din Yarr (Cardinia) Creek. He built a home of ti-tree and daub, erected the necessary yards and bought stock as he extended the clearing. As was often the case with our early settlers, he had left a wife and children 'at home' until he established a new place for them in Australia. Spare a thought for Mrs Patterson and her wee bairns in the swamps and ti-tree forest that covered most of the area.

Patterson was a pioneer in the true sense of the word. He opened up a new run in forbidding circumstances but maintained his good humour and hospitality at all times. Patterson also introduced the first Shorthorn cattle to the district, raised horses and sheep, was a well-known competitor at the ploughing competitions which were then very popular and was a driving force behind the Mornington Farmers' Society and the Dandenong Show Committee. After his death in 1896, his son, Thomas, carried on this interest and was on the committees of many farming and show organisations.

The next owner of 'St Germaine' was Joe McCormick, a retired Police Inspector. When he moved in, at about the turn of the century, he and his family made the homestead the social centre of the district. Yet memory is a strange thing. My mother went to the dances and parties arranged by the younger McCormicks. She must have marvelled at the Turkey-red carpets, the Nottingham lace curtains and the imported wallpapers, but the thing she remembers most clearly is the huge Coolgardie safe, large enough to hang a side of beef. Memory can be disturbingly unromantic at times!

The homestead was a graceful building. The wide verandas are supported by graceful and delicate cast-iron pillars. They were decorated with cast-iron lacework of great beauty which has, sadly, been removed. The bricks were all hand-made from clay dug on the property. These were the days of self-sufficiency. 'St Germaine' was more than a social centre; it was a cultural focus and a community centre.

The first post office in the area was opened in a front room of the house. It was run during the 20s and 30s by Katy McCormick, one of the daughters of 'Old Joe', but it has been closed for many years now.

The districts first school was opened in a cottage on the property, converted by the Education Department. It has long since gone but old army maps still show the school at Lisbaun, as it was called. Some road maps still show it as a town! While none of the older locals remember the origin of the name they do remember wading across the paddocks in winter to get to school. They remember Guy Dawson, the teacher, walking beside his bicycle because if he rode it the weight made it sink into the mud.

The property once extended well to the east of the Cardinia Creek which is now the boundary, the creek feeding a large system of lagoons which supported a great number of water-birds. Flooding was a regular winter situation and the roads were often impassable for weeks at a time.

Road names around 'St Germaine' reflect the history of the homestead. Pattersons Road was named for the first owner, possibly because there was no-one else to name it after. There is also a McCormicks Road. Pound Road, which links Narre Warren and Hampton Park, was once known as St Germaine Road and there is a movement afoot to change it back to that name.

The waterhole on the Cranbourne Road, known irreverently to some as Frog Hollow, was once St Germaine Lagoon. This was a popular and important watering-place and camp site. Now it is little more than a boggy waterhole but it was once large with a year-round water supply. There was a triangle of Crown land there for many years and a good supply of firewood. The slight rise also meant a dry camp, something of a rarity in those parts. Good camp sites were important in an age when it could take six days to travel from Dandenong to Lang Lang, or Tobin Yallock, as it was then known. This was partly due to the difficulty of passing through the Tooradin area.

Water was always a problem in one way or another. Every year the swamp flooded. Every year the roads were cut and 'St Germaine' was isolated. In 1898, however, the problem was a lack of water. Bushfires swept the area and the forests of the swamp were ablaze for weeks. The Clyde area escaped virtually undamaged and 'St Germaine' also escaped. The homestead was threatened by fire in 1944 but again it survived.

The history of 'St Germaine' goes back beyond Patterson, of course. On a sandy rise by the Cardinia Creek there is an Aboriginal burial ground. The mounds are still visible. Perhaps 'St Germaine' stands upon what was once sacred ground. We will never know, because the Bunurong, whose land this once was, were never a strong tribe and the coming of the white man spelt their doom. Gone, too, are the ducks and the lyrebirds.

Perhaps the homestead will one day be fully restored and at least a part of this history will be preserved.

13 How Young Bumper was Cheated of a Bullock-team

Bumper Gee is a real character in the old-time sense of the word. He usually has a yarn for every situation and, if he doesn't, he'll soon make up one. If you add to his lively imagination a good memory, the rich and varied experiences of a long and colourful life and the skill of a raconteur, the result is a goldmine of fascinating information.

Behind the talk, the jokes, the exaggeration, there is the grim reality faced by the first settlers on the Koo Wee Rup Swamp. In the days when Bumper's people moved onto the swamp it was a vast and forbidding morass. The dense ti-tree stretched for hundreds of square kilometres, all but impenetrable. Flooding was an annual event and even clearing a home site was a task for giants.

Bumper's father and his first wife came to Australia in the *Duke of Devonshire* in 1884. The ship berthed in Brisbane and, within a matter of days, the young couple were heading west. They had arranged jobs at Roma, he as a station rouseabout and she as a cook.

Mrs Gee was never to reach Roma. She contracted an unidentifiable illness and the doctor travelling with their party was unable to save her. They were five days out of Roma when she died and the heat was intense, so she was buried on a sheet of bark by the roadside. Her grave is one of the many unmarked resting places in which our pioneers often lie.

Understandably, Roma held no attraction for her husband. He couldn't settle down and soon sailed to New Zealand to make a fresh start. There, two years later, he met and married the girl who was to be Bumper's mother.

Bumper was born in Petone, New Zealand, in 1887. His given name was Harold but for as long as anyone can remember he has been called Bumper. The family came to Melbourne soon after and Bumper can remember Fitzgerald's circus in the open paddock at Princes Bridge in 1891 or 1892.

In the 1890s the banks in Melbourne were in dire straits; the economic climate became very bad and there were many unemployed. Mr Gee was one of a carriage-load of unemployed men who were sent to Drouin to seek work, eventually going to Red Hill, west of the town, to cut timber. There Bumper first met George Patten, whose bullock team carried the wood to the railway for transport to Melbourne. The scheme was doomed to failure from the outset. With the building trade at a standstill there was simply no demand for timber. The men now had work but they still had no income.

It was at this time that Bumper suffered his first rebuff in a long career of entertainment. Patten jokingly told the six-year-old boy that he would give him the bullock-team if he sang a few songs. Bumper 'sang for hours' but Patten kept the team.

The scheme under which the men came to Drouin was the Tucker Village Settlement Scheme. It was thought the scheme was named for a member of Parliament but Mr Hearn, of Longwarry, later said it was named after a Canon Tucker of the Church of England. The settlement workers, now virtually unemployed again, were given a tent and each week they were issued basic rations, including two litres of molasses. 'Confounded treacle!' Bumper still calls it. 'I've never eaten it since and I reckon I can still taste it!'

Bumper's father was a bootmaker by trade 'and a proper bootmaker. You could take him a piece of leather and he'd do the whole job from there on.' He took to collecting boots that needed repair and bringing them home to work on at night in the tent. This helped keep body and soul together for a few months and then he opened a 'Booty's' in Longwarry, which was then a thriving little community.

Bumper remembers Collins' horse team bringing in timber for the sawmills in Longwarry. They brought loads in from as far away as twenty-six kilometres — not a bad day's work for a team. Then the Koo Wee Rup drainage works started and part of the scheme involved settlers moving onto the supposedly drained land. The Gees moved onto a block of eight hectares on the Modella Road. Their neighbours were the Morecombes, Bensons, Lowes, Humphries and Cliffords.

Top: James and Maggie Pennycuick (see Story 9).
Bottom: The original Pennycuick home at Budgeree (see Story 9)

Top: The Warragul Railway Station (see Story 10).
Bottom: The Railway Hotel, Warragul (see Story 10).
Photo: Country Roads Board, Victoria

It was soon apparent that eight hectares was not nearly enough to support a family. Bumper claims it was the poorest land in Australia. There were only two and a half centimetres of topsoil and then the subsoil was a hard white clay which fiercely resisted all attempts to break it up. They stayed on their block only a few months.

While they were on the block they suffered a tragedy which seems amusing now but must have been deadly serious in those difficult days. In return for a pair of boots a settler gave them a goat. The following morning Bumper awoke to the sound of violent swearing and sticks being thrown against the wall. He emerged to find his father hurling sticks and abuse at the goat which had, during the night, eaten the ends off all the washing on the line. Most of their clothes were ruined beyond repair.

In 1895 they obtained a block at Iona. For months, Bumper never saw his father. He was gone at 5.00 a.m. to walk down to Iona to continue clearing the new block and he was never home until well after dark. Toward the end of that year the whole family walked down to their new home.

It was at about this time that they became friendly with the Hobson family. Later, one of his sisters was to marry into the family. Ted Hobson had been at Iona for some time and had cleared most of his block. His house was made of ti-tree but it had an iron roof, the iron being delivered to the school, as far as a horse and cart could go, then carried down to the house one sheet at a time.

At this stage most of the men were also working on the drains. The pay was £4 per week and the men spent every second week on the drains and the rest of the time on their farms. Some of the farms were on perpetual lease but this was not a popular scheme, as such farms were never really the property of the farmer. The 'conditional lease' (whereby the farmer bought the farm, conditional upon maintaining a certain scale of improvements) was far more popular because the men had a sense of ownership and this helped create a pride in their properties and a little more incentive to work.

The farms were bought at £5 per acre with interest at four and a half per cent over forty years. This was a very high rate of interest in those days but a deputation which went to Melbourne to seek a lowering of the interest rate was unsuccessful.

14 How Bumper Lost the Calves' Milk

Some people look back to the good old days; some people call them the bad old days. In truth, the bad old days had a lot of good in them and the good old days had a lot of bad in them. One of the bad things Bumper Gee remembers was coming home from the butter factory without any milk for the calves.

Back in the years just after the turn of the century there were many small farmers around Iona who kept cows on their small properties. It soon became obvious that the standard block size of eight hectares was not enough for a dairy herd, but, in the meantime, there was a minor boom in the industry which led to there being three butter factories within two kilometres of each other along the Main Drain.

The first was probably the Fresh Food and Frozen Storage Company's factory on the 'fifteen-mile', on Jack George's block. Bumper's father was taking milk there in 1898 and it had been running for about two years before that. At this time, Cora Lynn did not exist. Settlers had begun to clear their small blocks at Iona but Cora Lynn was still no more than a ti-tree wilderness. There was no settlement there until about 1900.

Bumper's father took quite a time to clear his block. When there was grass in the clearing he began to buy cows and by the end of 1898 the Gees owned six or seven head. The milk was taken up the track to the factory in a wheelbarrow. This was the standard method of milk transport in those days on the Great Swamp. Each wheelbarrow had a strap between the shafts which fitted over the shoulders of the unfortunate bearer to help spread the weight. The barrow was then pushed and pulled the four kilometres to the factory.

Now, these were not really butter factories. They were separation plants at which each farmer would tip his milk into a large vat.

The milk went through a separator and the farmer collected the appropriate quantity of skimmed milk in the cans he'd used to bring in his whole milk. In this way each farmer supposedly obtained a fair share of the skimmed milk, which was important as a calf and pig food. If you put in two cans of whole milk you got back two cans of skimmed milk, but there wasn't any accurate measuring device and a few 'smart ones' soon woke up to the fact that cans could be taken in only half or three-quarters full and taken home completely filled. This meant, of course, that someone had to miss out in the end. It was usually young Bumper who found that, when he finally got a chance to put his cans under the spout, there simply wasn't any skimmed milk left in the vat.

His father was 'not amused'.

Bumper and one of his friends solved this problem by taking their milk in very early, often being at the factory at sunrise even in the summer. In this way they got back their full measure of skimmed milk before the rush, but it also meant that they would sometimes have to start milking at three o'clock in the morning.

The cream was sent from the factory by horse and cart to meet the daily 'milk train' which took it to Melbourne. Some factories only sent the cream down every second day but no-one seemed to mind. Not so long ago a primary school arithmetic book included problems relating to the number of cream cans picked up by the train at stations between Warragul and Dandenong. Another thing Bumper recalls well is the number of inventions farmers came up with to help get their milk to the separators. There were two-wheeled barrows, three-wheeled barrows and even double-decker barrows.

To add to Bumper's problems, his father arranged to take in and deliver milk for the neighbours at one shilling per can per week. Remember that Bumper was only thirteen years old at the time and the factory was four kilometres away over a rough and muddy track. Fortunately, after six months of this extra work, his father bought a horse and Bumper survived.

Then the 'Marchbanks Patent' saved him from the plunderers who once sent him home without any milk for the calves. This was a device which measured the flow of the skimmed milk. Under the old system the milk came out in a continuous flow but with the

Marchbanks Patent, as it was always known, the manager could set a scale to release only the amount to which each farmer was entitled and everybody got a fair go.

When the farmer arrived at the factory, he'd haul his cans up to the second storey of the building and tip them into a vat which held about 2,000 or 2,300 litres. This was heated by steam from a small steam engine to speed up the process. The engine, which also drove the separator, was of about 5 h.p.

Bumper remembers the Vervale butter factory, or creamery, operated by Holdenson and Neilson. It was at the corner where the Vervale store stood later, but it lasted only a couple of years before it closed. At the turn of the century only the very largest farms produced ninety litres or so, and there simply wasn't the volume of milk to justify three factories. This was in the days when the government thought that eight hectares was enough to support a dairy farmer and his family.

The Fresh Food and Frozen Storage Company closed down in about 1902 (The Holdenson and Nielsen Vervale plant was opened later than the others, in about 1905.) The Drouin Butter Factory opened a creamery at Cora Lynn in about 1906 under the management of a Mr Wakenshaw. This prospered until about 1925. At the Cora Lynn end of the district the farms were larger and more economically viable; the Cora Lynn creamery also had a cooperative store attached.

On the smaller allotments at the Iona end the potato soon proved itself a much better proposition and the creameries were forced out of business. Potato-growing was an ideal source of income. The ground had never been cultivated before and the area in which Bumper's father farmed at Iona had a light, fluffy soil that was easy to work. Bumper's father worked along with a hoe, half-lifting one sod at a time and then dropping it back into place as soon as Bumper threw a seed potato into the hole. It was a crude system but it worked.

Another memory which has survived is that of the Kellys. There was 'Gentleman Kelly', 'Kelly the Rake', 'Ned Kelly', 'Stuttering Kelly' and 'Spitting Kelly'. Each had a characteristic which earned him his own peculiar nickname. 'Old Spittin' Kelly', Bumper said. 'Well, I tell yer, yer 'ad ter stand a good way from 'im ter talk ter 'im. 'E 'ad a funny way of speakin' an' 'e'd spray yer every time!'

15 Too Roo Dun—Monster Man-eater

Was there a strange monster in the waters of Western Port? The Aborigines believed that a fabulous man-eating monster lived in a deep hole somewhere near Tooradin. Whether or not this was true, the white men who first came to the area used the natives' name, 'Too Roo Dun', for the monster, though they spelt it 'Tooradin' when the town was finally surveyed.

Possibly William Hovell, the ill-fated explorer, was the first white man to see the Tooradin area during his unhappy search for 'the plains of Iramoo'. In 1839 permanent settlement was coming closer to Tooradin with the taking up of the Yallock Run by Robert Jamieson and Sam Rawson. We know that the Manton brothers, Frederick and Charles, took up the Tooradin Run in 1840 and that they purchased it from Edwin Sawtells, a merchant with property interests after whom Sawtells Inlet is named. It was in that same year that the Polish adventurer and opportunist, Paul Strzelecki, wandered into Tooradin. Local legend has it that he had been hopelessly lost in the hills that now bear his name and had been assisted by escaped convicts from the abandoned Corinella settlement.

In 1846 the Mantons sold their licence to J. Akins. It later passed to R. V. Clarke and then, in 1850, to John Pike. John Mickle, William Lyall and John Bakewell purchased the run in 1852 and added it to their gigantic Western Port Stations combine. The Western Port Stations partnership was amicably dissolved in 1857 and the 'Tooradin Plains' became the property of John Bakewell. Lyall kept the land east of the Inlet.

In February 1854, the present township site was surveyed by a government surveyor called Foot. The Inlet was already being used as a small port for the bringing in of supplies to the local stations at Harewood, Yallock, Red Bluff and Tooradin. It would seem that the first subdivision on the village area was of about eight lots and these were sold in 1869. In April 1873 the Shire Council informed the Parliament that a jetty was needed at Tooradin because boats unloading goods had to wait for the next high tide to get away again, as the channel was a considerable distance from the shore. Much of the timber and stone used for the Western Port Road were also shipped into Tooradin because of the difficulty the swamps presented for wheeled traffic.

It is usually true that the building of a proper hotel conveys a degree of permanence on a small township. John Turner Steer opened his hotel in 1868 or 1869. It was run as an inn for about a year and was then licenced to sell beer. The present Bridge Hotel is on Steer's original site, which was Lot 8 of the first subdivision. Behind the hotel were many Aboriginal kitchen middens which lay undisturbed until quite recently.

In 1875 John Woodfield Thrupp apparently opened a store in the village. At about the same time a Mr Woolley opened a store opposite the hotel, the same gentleman being registered as Tooradin's first Postmaster on 13 August 1877. Soon after, he went bankrupt. The first doctor in the town was Hilsham, whose services were obtained following a public meeting called by William Lyall on 5 July 1876. That meeting began a fund to purchase a medicine chest, instruments, a saddle and a horse.

During the mid-1870s Tooradin was served by daily coach services to the 'big smoke'. The two companies providing this service were Cobb and Co and Usher's, the trip taking five and a half hours each way.

The Railways Commissioners visited Tooradin on 29 April 1885, as they were considering the route to be taken by the Great Southern Railway. The townspeople were jubilant but their enthusiasm was somewhat dampened by the discovery that the nearest station would be five kilometres north of the town.

The Dandenong-Tooradin section of the line was opened on 1 October 1888. On the same day, seven other railways in the State were opened. This was at the height of the boom that preceded the Depression of the 1890s. The contractor was Jonathan Falkingham, who worked a team of 280 men, with sixty-two horses, sixteen wagons and three bullock teams. They fought an almost hopeless battle with the wet weather and the swamps but the line was opened on time.

By 1865 it was possible to leave Melbourne at either 6.50 a.m. or 5.00 p.m. for Tooradin. The morning trip was scheduled to take one hour and forty-eight minutes and the evening trip took two hours and seventeen minutes. This was obviously faster than the coach and more comfortable but the traveller was still faced with the terrible journey down Tooradin Station Road to the township. This road was incredibly bad for many years.

The Tooradin bridge over Sawtells Inlet has become a landmark. It was apparently first erected in the 1850s; until then cattle were taken around the head of the Inlet. Cranbourne Shire records show that the bridge was in need of repair in 1871 and that a contractor named Smethurst had carried out the repair by September 1873. In 1903 the Shire minutes show that the bridge was again out of service. In June of that year a tender was let to Turnbull Brothers for the building of a dam across the Inlet, instead of a full bridge. This was opened in 1904 and that was apparently when the first 'flood gates' were installed.

When the hotel was first opened in about 1868-69, John Turner Steer called it the Tooradin Inn. There was also a Sherwood Hotel in the township at about the same time. Steer died in 1876 and in 1877 a Mr M. Evans was advertising accommodation at the Tooradin Hotel. A later publican, Thomas John Thompson, renamed it the Bridge Hotel. James Dudley Singleton reverted to the original name when he became the licencee in February 1917.

The Sherwood Hotel was also known as the Robin Hood but it apparently had no connection with the Robin Hood in Drouin. It appears that it was built by a Mr M. Stephens in 1869. In March 1878 the licencee, J. L. Strudwick, had died and the licence was transferred to the Poole family. At this time it had eleven rooms, with a bar, kitchen, five detached rooms, a stable and a buggy house. It was built on two lots totalling 104 hectares.

The Tooradin garage was opened in 1920, reflecting the importance of Tooradin as a stop on the road to South Gippsland and Phillip Island. The site was bought from Alice Mickle by John Colvin and Sons. When they built the garage it was managed by Gordon Lyall for a time and then he and his brother, Harewood Lyall, became the proprietors.

Another connection with motoring lies in the fact that the Royal Automobile Club of Victoria was 'born' at Tooradin. Apparently

Harry B. James, Sydney Day and J. G. Coleman drove down from Melbourne in May 1903. The difficulties they saw facing the motorist on the trip convinced them that a branch of the Royal Automobile Club was needed in Victoria.

16 The Disappearing Schoolroom

Could you still find your way to your early school? Many of those schools that served West Gippslanders in the past have now disappeared or have been moved to new locations.

They were temporary affairs at best, with classes conducted in bark huts and spare rooms by teachers whose qualifications left much to be desired (though some of them were excellent teachers). Many served mining camps or railway construction crews and these disappeared as reefs ran out or the railway moved on. The histories of these transient schools are poorly documented and in many cases the schools were 'unofficial'.

One school with a colourful history is Pakenham Consolidated School. The Roman Catholic Church opened a school in Pakenham on 27 January 1862. Operating under the control of the Denominational Schools Board it was to function until 1868. A State School was opened in January 1875, on a site of about one hectare somewhere on the banks of the Toomuc Creek. This school ran half-time with Cardinia (then known as Pakenham South). In 1891 it became a full-time school and moved to the Main Street site now occupied by the Pakenham Consolidated School.

In May 1951, the school that had begun on the banks of a creek in the middle of nowhere became the huge Pakenham Consolidated School, swallowing up eleven small schools in the surrounding district. The schools to disappear were Tynong, Toomuc Valley, Rythdale, Mount Burnett, Pakenham Upper, Pakenham South, Nar Nar Goon South, Nar Nar Goon North, Cora Lynn, Army Road and Tynong North.

The shortest-lived schools of all were usually associated with mining settlements. In the Walhalla area, Pearson Town school opened in about 1873 and was closed in 1881. Coppermine opened in March 1879, and was moved to Pearson Town in 1883. It closed again in 1888 and re-opened in 1889 — only to be burnt down in a bushfire in 1893. This time it stayed closed.

Buildings were shifted around almost as much in those days as they are now. The second classroom at Beaconsfield was originally part of the Narre Warren school. Around Walhalla and Woods Point, this regular shifting was necessary. When the men moved to another 'strike', taking their families with them, the school often moved too.

The Walhalla school was shifted because it was too close to the crushers at the Long Tunnel Mine. The teachers could not be heard, even when they shouted. Before this the situation had been confused by there being two schools, each claiming to be the official school, with two Headmasters, each claiming to be the official Headmaster and each claiming a State salary. The first school was eventually burnt down on 25 April 1891. The rebuilt school was closed in 1952, re-opened in 1955 and closed again in 1959.

If this seems a chequered career it pales into insignificance beside the experience of the Tanjil school. In 1870 a private school at Tanjil gained official recognition and became Tanjil Rural School No. 40, with John Ward appointed as Headmaster. Ward was not terribly interested in running a day school, however, and conducted a night school instead. Amazingly, it was nearly three years before a District Inspector visited the school and discovered this strange state of affairs. The Tanjil school was re-opened in April 1875, on a new site, in a new building and, not surprisingly, with a new teacher. By 1898 a dwindling population had forced the closure of the school.

Another fly-by-night school was at Store Point, about thirty-two kilometres north of Walhalla. Store Point opened in 1871 and closed in 1899. There was another school nearby called Edwards Reef. The teacher at Edwards Reef was told to operate the two schools on a half-time basis. He claimed that two and a half kilometres was too great a distance to travel in such rugged country but the Education Department was adamant that the two schools should share the one teacher. The teacher, Davenport, ignored the Department and closed the Edwards Reef school on his own authority!

Earlier I mentioned Pakenham Consolidated School. Poowong Consolidated School is another giant which has swallowed its smaller neighbours. The Poowong school was opened on 2 December 1878, and shifted to a new site in 1903. In 1945, after four years of negotiations with the School committees concerned, Ranceby, Bell View and Poowong South schools were closed and their pupils transferred to Poowong. In 1949 Poowong was declared a 'Group School'. There were moves to attract other local schools but only Mount Lyall joined the group. This was in 1951.

There is also a Consolidated School at Red Hill and another at Foster. The original Foster school opened on 13 November 1871. The District Inspector reported that there would be between thirty and fifty pupils attending, with 'rather fewer in winter as no roads have yet been formed'.

In 1873 the Headmaster reported that the school had been undermined by the gold and tin mining along the creek so a new site was purchased on Cement Hill, now known as Church Hill. There was a dispute over this site, for some reason, and the present site was then purchased. At first, the site used was only about one fifth of a hectare, but more land was added in 1882, 1889, 1902 and again in 1960.

There were countless smaller schools which disappeared over the years. The original Nar Nar Goon school was renamed Pakenham East. It was opened in 1874 and closed in 1891. Sherwood, near Tooradin, opened on 28 April 1878, and closed on 28 February 1882, only eight years later. Queensferry lasted a little longer, operating between 17 March 1876, and 1883.

Some have died since the Second World War. Hazelwood was opened in October 1876, and was not closed until the State Electricity Commission wanted the site in 1945. Garfield North closed recently and Tonimbuk, opened in 1899, closed in 1947.

But what of the really old ones? Who has ever heard of Red Jacket school, near Woods Point, (1871-1899), Back Beach school on Phillip Island (1871-1878), Lisbaun school on 'St Germaine' at Clyde (1926-1937), Woranga school near Tarraville (1875-1893), Rock Cutting school near Drouin (1880-1886), Oslers Creek or Toomboon schools (1884-1897 and 1885-1907 respectively) near Walhalla, or the Star of Hope and Perseverance schools on French Island, dating from about 1896?

17 The Noojee Rail Link—An Engineering Classic

The railway from Neerim South to Noojee swoops and soars through some of Victoria's most attractive scenery. Unfortunately, most of the trestle bridges carrying the line over deep fern gullies have been burnt out. The cost of rebuilding them appears to be prohibitive and it seems that Noojee will never again hear the whistle of a locomotive.

The history of the line tends to fall into two parts. The line from Warragul to Neerim South was built with little difficulty, though there were many embankments and cuttings to be built in the foothills of the ranges. From Neerim South to Noojee was a vastly different terrain and the way in which the engineers conquered these steep slopes, dense forest and deep gullies, is a classical example of determined and imaginative engineering.

Warragul station, the southern terminus, was built by T. Cockram and Company under a contract dated 17 May 1878. The contract price of £3,403 6s was apparently adhered to and the station was opened in 1879. There were only two rough sheds and an earth platform to serve the needs of the Stationmaster and passengers.

These were the days of the railway boom and residents of the Warragul district soon began to agitate for a line north into the hills. Some also wanted a line running south into the Leongatha area, but this never gained much support. The Government did, however, agree to build a line north of the town to the dairying and timber areas of Neerim and Noojee. The contract for the first stage of the line, to run from Warragul to Rokeby, was let to J. Ahearn. He agreed to build thirteen kilometres of track for £52,880. This first stage was fairly straightforward and was opened, on schedule, on 12 May 1890.

The contract for the second stage, from Rokeby to Neerim South, was let to M. Govan on 12 September 1890. Govan was unable to begin the work and the contract passed to B. Wallace. The price agreed to was £26,948. This section was opened on 18 March 1892. The total capital cost as far as Neerim South came to £123,469. This included such items as the purchase of land, the building of bridges and buildings, culverts and the like. By 1919 it cost only 2s 11d to make the return journey from Warragul to Neerim South.

Thus far the line had posed few engineering problems, but Neerim South lies on the foothills of the Baw Baw Ranges and the next sections of the line ran through very steep country. So far the line had climbed from the flat country near Warragul to Neerim South, but now it began a much more difficult ascent. The 'summit' was reached about three quarters of a kilometre out of Nayook, on the Noojee side. Then began a precipitous descent to the timber town. This 'summit' was 431 metres above sea level, 325 metres above Warragul. At times the gradients on the last section were as steep as 1 in 30.

The section to Nayook was opened on 27 March 1917. It had cost £79,796. Construction had begun in 1913 but the First World War had meant a labour shortage for many public works, including railway building. It cost a further £45,832 to extend the line down into Noojee. This section was opened in April 1919. The opening brought the total capital cost of the line to £258,766. The descent from Nayook wound around steep spurs and was carried over the gullies on a series of trestle bridges that was probably without equal in the State. Sadly, fire has destroyed all but one.

The grades between Nayook and Noojee were sometimes 1 in 37. There were seven major trestle bridges, with a total length of more than 460 metres. The station was built on the slope above the town because bringing it into the township itself would have entailed a much steeper grade than trains could handle. The site of the Noojee station was on land originally selected by Messrs Riddell and Taylor. A turntable was built because there was not enough flat land for a turning loop.

The first station master was J. A. Wilson, but his appointment was not effective until 23 November 1926. He stayed until 3 August 1930. Caretakers then managed the station until 1940. A 'porter-in-charge' was appointed on 31 July 1940. He was H. A. Stewart and he stayed until 1951 when the station reverted to 'caretaker' status. It was closed in 1954.

In the 1920s a market-day train ran to Warragul and back every Thursday, but most of the traffic on the line was timber being sent to Melbourne. Peak revenue for the line was nearly £34,000, earned in 1922-23. In 1929 only 230 passengers were carried. Other traffic included two truckloads of dray horses, seven truckloads of beef and dairy cattle and twelve truckloads of sheep for the butcher.

1930 saw the end of the market-day train, though a daily goods service was continued. During 1936-39 the goods service was reduced to one train each Monday, Wednesday and Friday. By 1943 this had increased again to a twice-daily service because of the heavy wartime demands for timber. On Sundays there were three trains.

The Nayook-Noojee section was closed three times. A fire in 1926 destroyed the Noojee station and one of the trestles, and the line was closed for three months while repairs were carried out. In 1938 fire claimed another bridge and this time the line was closed for two months.

The great fires of 1939 again destroyed the station and this time most of the town went with it. All the bridges and culverts on the northern section were destroyed or damaged. It seemed that Noojee had been dealt a deathblow. A train in the Noojee yards managed to escape the flames. The driver was ordered to take his train out as the fires closed in; as a result he and the firemen had to inspect every bridge on foot before taking the train across.

It wasn't a deathblow for the town. Noojee is more determined than the Phoenix. On 3 March 1954, a special train took people along the line into Warragul to meet the Royal Train, carrying Queen Elizabeth and Prince Phillip. This train had five passenger carriages, making it the longest passenger train the line had ever seen.

Shortly after, another bridge was destroyed by fire and the line was finally closed. Now people are beginning to think of it as a tourist railway. It passes through magnificent scenery and, if it ever was opened again, would surely attract as many passengers now as it ever did during normal operation in the past.

18 Cranbourne Sets Its Own Pace

Cranbourne is an independent community. Somehow it seems to continue on at its own pace, making its own decisions, whatever pressures are applied by the rapid development of the region.

Development brings crisis to most towns; if it has done so in Cranbourne, the crises are well hidden. Perhaps in Cranbourne the independent spirit of the early settlers still leads an independent life.

Cranbourne township came into existence officially on 18 March 1852, when the first sale of township allotments was made in Melbourne. The area had been surveyed earlier in the year by H. B. Foot. Even then, it was a hardly a 'township' survey. Most of the blocks were quite large, ranging in size from twelve to 257 hectares. The Towbeet, Mayune and Barker's Heifer Stations were broken up, with the owners having a pre-emptive right to 259 hectares each.

At the same time land was being surveyed and sold at Narre Warren and Dandenong. The Lands Office had to find names for the new areas and settled on the names of British Lords. In this way Lords Lyndhurst, Cranborne and Longford (Pakenham) all gained a measure of immortality but, unfortunately for Lord 'Cranborne, some clerk inadvertently added a 'u' to his name.

Some of the families who bought land at these early sales are still represented in the district. Among the first arrivals was Colin Crilhie Clarke, who arrived late in the 1840s and took up 'Beaulieu'. He raised his own grapes and made his own wine from them. Clarke's wife was Margaret Fagan, an Irish girl who added much to the colour and the history of the area. She grew up in Clonvaraghan and saw her father and brother sail away to the new south land. Later they sent for the remainder of the family and Margaret's mother bought them passages on the *Earl of Charlemont* which was wrecked on the voyage out. All the passengers were saved but their possessions were lost.

Four years later, in 1857, Margaret's father died. Her mother opened a shanty at Fagan's Hill, now the site of the Radio Australia transmitter at Lyndhurst. She soon established a wide reputation among travellers for her honesty and generosity.

Margaret married Colin Crilhie Clarke and the other two daughters also married local settlers, Hall and Nelson. The Fagan sons also seem to have farmed in the area although there is no record of their having obtained land of their own. The Fagans settled around Lyndhurst but other farmers were already moving further to the south and east, into the low hills bordering the Great Swamp. Clyde and Cranbourne areas were being opened up at this time.

Anthony Ridgway was fairly typical of these early farmers. They were men who would try anything once — and often had to. He came from Buckinghamshire to Melbourne in 1849. At first he farmed at Moonee Ponds but then moved to Ballarat. Hearing of good soil in the Clyde area, he came to have a look and soon purchased 126 hectares. There he kept a dairy herd, pigs, bees, raised pedigreed stock which he exhibited very successfully, and founded what may well be called a dynasty.

Other names in the Clyde area at the time were Sykes, Atkinson, Leamon, Close, Werritt, Wisewould and Sleeth. In the Lyndhurst area there were the Birds, the Dunlops, the Howards, the Simes and the Halls. Further north, in the Eummemmerring area, the names included Garner, Kirkham, Legg, Lord and Keys.

Of these the Kirkham's were perhaps the most colourful. The first Kirkham here was a ship's carpenter who 'jumped ship' with two friends while their boat was anchored in the Yarra. They swam across the river and made good their escape, except that they spent the night in a tree hiding from some dreadful monster which turned out, in the cold, grey light of dawn, to be a cow. Kirkham eventually settled near Dandenong and four of his grandsons became noted sportsmen. Don Kirkham became a world champion cyclist. Another grandson became a champion rifleman. As Lieutenant Max Kirkham, he made the supreme sacrifice in the First World War.

The closer allocation of titles in the area resulting from the land sales in 1852 brought more settlers and a greater demand for residential and other small blocks. The township area of Cranbourne was surveyed again in 1856. There was already a small but secure community on the site.

One member of this small community was the Reverend Alexander Duff. He was to exercise a remarkable influence, helped, no doubt, by the fact that many of the settlers were what he called 'guid Scots Presbyterians'. Duff had a Master's Degree from Glasgow University but his influence in the growing Cranbourne area came from qualifications of a different kind.

He was a truly Christian gentleman who believed that a clergyman should lead his flock, rather than direct it. He was instrumental in bringing about the situation whereby, only eight years after the second survey, the church, manse and school in Cranbourne were free of debt and completely furnished. He also began moves for the building of a school at Bass. He preached throughout the area bounded by Dandenong, the Bass Valley, the Great Swamp, Berwick and Cranbourne.

Duff was also a competent ploughman and maintained his own team with which he entered the ploughing competitions popular at the time. He experimented with various methods of improving the quality of cheese made in the area. Though very much a practising preacher he was found more often with his sleeves rolled up than with them down.

The schools in Cranbourne naturally followed the growth of the town. These have been well-documented and are a boon to historians. There was a Church of England school at Lyndhurst in 1854. There was a Roman Catholic school there in 1857, which a District Inspector described as 'Very dirty, dusty and unhealthy'. In 1858 a new Roman Catholic school was built beside the church reserve in Cranbourne. The Presbyterian School in Cranbourne was built in 1856. There was another a Clyde in 1858.

Now Cranbourne is moving ahead rapidly, but nearly all the development, from the racecourse to the several new schools, is being controlled by locals who are, in many cases, descended from those hardy settlers who moved a little further out to find land for themselves and a future for their children.

19 Wonthaggi—Black Gold and Tourist Dollars

The coal mines of Wonthaggi may soon become a major Victorian tourist attraction if one active group of residents has its way. The mines that once yielded high-quality black coal may yield tourist dollars instead. In financial terms they may be more successful than they ever were while operating as mines, but they will never surpass their general importance to Victoria in the first decades of the twentieth century.

The assurance of a continuous and reliable source of brown coal was essential for the operation of our railways. Those railways, in turn, were vital to the continuing development of the State, particularly in the days before road transport became fast and economical.

Without Wonthaggi coal the railways would have come, at times, to a standstill. Without the railways, our development, at least in rural areas, may well have done the same.

The Wonthaggi Historical Society has among its treasures a copy of the *Annual Report of the General Manager of the State Coal Mines* made in 1914. The report provides an excellent picture of the importance of the mines. The manager was then George H. Broome, his report being dated 24 September 1914. It was submitted to the Honourable Donald Mackinnon, M.P., Minister for Railways. Section 93 of the Coal Mines Act of 1909 required the manager to report to both Houses of Parliament annually. Any member of the public who wished to see the report could purchase a copy for one shilling.

The output of the State Mine (or mines) was 510490 tonnes for the year; the total quantity available to the State was 495155 tonnes. The difference was lost in wastage and in sales to miners and other local residents. Three quarters of the output was sold to the Victorian Railways.

It is ironic that there is a certain amount of rivalry between the supporters of the Coal Creek Historical Park at Korumburra and those supporting the State Mine Historical Park at Wonthaggi. The irony lies in the fact that it was sales to the Victorian Railways that made the Powlett coalfields at Wonthaggi a success — yet it was Korumburra coal which established the quality and calorific value of Gippsland black coal for railway use. Coal from Wonthaggi was, incidentally, trucked to Korumburra to 'dress up' the opening of the Coal Creek venture.

A miners' strike at Newcastle in 1910 severely restricted the supply of coal to Victoria. Until then, nearly all the coal used in Victoria was shipped around the coast from Newcastle. The strike made it clear the Victoria must have its own supply and it was decided to develop the Powlett coalfields.

Even then, there were industrial disputes which affected coal production but the report seems to indicate that management and labour were able to negotiate with greater success in those days than now. The report says: '. . . the mine lost 16 days through disputes ... the longest stoppage was 7 days and was caused by the dismissal for incompetency of a number of wheelers and the action of the other wheelers in leaving their work in sympathy ... Their action was not upheld by the Miners Union [which] gave an undertaking that the

Top: Mixed goods at Nyora (see Story 11).
Bottom: 'St Germaine', Koo Wee Rup Swamp (see Story 12)

Top: 'Caldermeade' homestead, between Tooradin and Lang Lang (see Story 15).
Bottom: The old Cowes school

mine would not again be thrown idle by a similar action ... This undertaking has been loyally observed.'

In the same year six days were lost through fatal accidents. Three fatalities were caused by falls of stone at the working face and one was caused by a machinery accident on the surface. This was shaft mining and not open-cut, so falls were a constant hazard.

The mine worked 253 days in the financial year July 1913 to June 1914. The average daily earnings of the miners came to 13s 11 $\frac{1}{2}$d, so average annual incomes must have been about £175. This was a reasonable income in those days but hardly one which compensated the miners for the constant dirt, danger and discomfort of shaft mining. About three quarters of the miners worked underground. In 1914 the average number of employees was 1011. Of these, 457 were miners, ninety were wheelers, 165 had other underground jobs and 299 were employed on the surface.

Men and horses were still essential underground but much of the actual coal-cutting was done by machines. There were twenty-three coal-cutting machines in use in 1914 and they were proving very satisfactory. Still, the books show that in 1913 horses and harness cost £2,001 4s. In 1914 the cost was £1948 13s 9d. The difficulty the manager had in running a profitable operation was partly due to the fact that the Mines Department rented the land to the State Coal Mine at a fee of £500 per annum and another £4,000 was used to purchase other land. As well as this, the Treasury advanced the Railways £6,600 to pay for coal cartage — and the State Coal Mine had to pay the debt! Despite all this the State Coal Mine showed a profit for the 1913-14 financial year of £1,212 19s.

The State Coal Mine was the raison d'etre of Wonthaggi and the sole arbiter of Wonthaggi's prosperity. Now it may well be the source of another boom.

20 Yannathan School—
Reflection of the Community

The history of the local school is quite often a reflection of the history of any community. Yannathan is no exception to this rule.

Information shows the development of the area from a ti-tree-covered swamp to the established farming community that it is today.

Settlers came from the western side of the Great Swamp in 1875. By the end of 1878 most of the land had been taken up but few settlers had been able to do much clearing.

The first Yannathan school was opened in 1878. It was later used as a residence for Primary School No. 2422, Yannathan. Another school building was brought from the corner of O'Shea's Road and North Road. Yannathan Primary School No. 2422, began in 1882 in a private house. It was run by John B. Heward who divided his time between two schools, the other being at Yannathan South. One of these part-time schools was near the present store and the other was near the recreation ground. The Yannathan school now running was built in 1890.

Yannathan South Primary School was opened on 2 October 1882. Parents had applied for a school in October of the previous year. This little school was later amalgamated with Yannathan when the new school was built in 1890. The present Yannathan South Primary School has no connection with the original of the name. It was opened under the name of Protectors Flat in 1895. The name was changed to Heath Hill in 1914 and in 1951 it became Yannathan South. Many locals still cling to the name of Heath Hill.

Yannathan Upper was opened in 1883 as Lang Lang North. It was on the south side of the Lang Lang Road but was moved to the north side in 1885. It was totally destroyed by a bushfire in 1892, reopened in 1895, renamed Yannathan Upper in 1906 and closed in 1912.

The first Headmaster at Yannathan Primary School No. 2422, (the present Yannathan school) was a Mr Scott but his successor made a much greater impression on the community. This was J. Denholm, who was a keen gardener and did a great deal to improve the school grounds. He also worked from the time of his arrival in 1899 to make the school a more integral part of the community.

Jessie Allen was a pupil-teacher at the school. In 1907 she married Denholm. Sixteen years later her husband succumbed to a sudden illness and was buried after a funeral attended by almost the entire population of the area. He left his wife with two daughters, Marjorie and Lynn.

Denholm had also been the Postmaster. He ran the post office in the porch of the school, but his successor as Headmaster, Mr Jeffrey, refused to take on the responsibility for the mails. A Mr McKay became the new Postmaster.

Greaves Brothers had already donated a 'pony paddock' to the school (pony races to and from the waterhole were a popular pastime during lunch hours) and now they built a two-roomed post office and bank. Mr Adeney, a bank manager at Koo Wee Rup, came over for a few hours each week to conduct the bank, and eventually it was taken over by the English, Scottish and Australian Bank at Lang Lang.

Constant flooding, particularly before the Lang Lang River was straightened, meant that many families had to use a buggy to get their children to school with dry feet. One enterprising farmer sent his five children to school on a draught horse! In 1922 the use of horses led to a tragedy. Una Mary Peck, seven years old, was thrown from a horse and killed while on her way to school.

The school records mention trips to the zoo and many picnics, and the Yannathan Recreation Reserve was often used by the school, being a vital community facility. The first committee for the reserve was formed in 1944 and they ensured that the annual New Year's Day sports became a great attraction.

Other dates found in the records are those relating to the Public Hall. Until it was built all public meetings and functions were held in one or other of the large lofts of barns in the district. As an example of the size of these, at a dinner held to celebrate the opening of the butter factory in 1900, one hundred settlers were seated in the loft at 'Parklands', the home of R. G. Gardiner. Mrs Sam Smethurst was, incidentally, granted the honour of switching on the new machinery at the butter factory.

The decision to build a hall was made in 1903. The farmers had soon erected a substantial building but it was destroyed by fire in 1932 and they had to build a new one. The first store was opened by Mr A. Alchin in 1879; the railway station was opened in June 1922, and the Union Church was the first public building to be erected.

The Honour Board in the school tells another tale and a more tragic one. There are fifty names on the board; of those nine made the supreme sacrifice. Remember that this was a very small community. W. H. Nelson and G. E. Harker each won a Military Medal.

An amusing tale which has survived the years is that of the McDonald family who moved down from Shepparton in 1902. They had to camp on the roadside at the Yallock Creek for six months while they built a bridge to obtain access to the property they had bought!

The name 'Lineham' crops up many times in the records. One noticeable mention is that of Willie Lineham, who set a record by never missing a day of school in seven years. Did he like school, one wonders, or was he perhaps more afraid of his father than of his teacher?

21 Mount Worth as a Symbol

Mount Worth has been a symbol of homecoming to Ellinbank people for many years. To those early settlers who cleared the forests the mountain was a beacon, standing proud and clear against the skyline. Its reach toward the sky provided, perhaps, an analogue for the task they faced.

Mount Worth is the highest peak of the tumbled Strzelecki Range; on one side there is a plantation of pines that has become a landmark in itself. The mountain was named after Richard Worth, who settled there in 1878. The names of other settlers are remembered in other ways.

The first known settler was John Hardie, who came to the district in 1874, one of many Scots who came to Gippsland in the 1870s. Born in Berwickshire, he was looking for a new land where there was room for a farmer who wanted to work his own soil. He and his wife, Ellen, had a daughter, Margaret, who was born before they came to Australia. Sadly, Ellen died in 1875 when the son, Alex, was born.

John Hardie later remarried and had five more children. He died in 1894, by which time he had seen the district named after his wife. He named his property 'Ellen Bank' in her honour and it was at his home that the first post office was opened. Later, a spelling mistake in official records led to the name of the area becoming Ellinbank.

Other settlers to come into the damp and dismal forests southeast of Warragul at that time came up from Drouin and then turned south along Lardners Track, then east again along a blazed trail. This avoided most of the swamps south of Warragul but meant heavy going in the steep foothills of the Strzelecki Range. A Mrs

Symes kept a store and post office on Lardners Track and this was the jumping-off point.

The Cropley family has figured large in the history of Ellinbank. Ben Cropley was born at Quadring, in Lincolnshire, England. He was only seventeen when he came to Melbourne, joining his three brothers here in the year 1850. They carted goods to the goldfields for a few years and then took up land at Werribee. Soon they heard there was good land to be had to the south of Warragul. In 1875, Ben and his brother Effield, with their nephews William, John and Alfred, moved into the area.

Three more nephews later joined them and this provided the base for a powerful family unit. One of the nephews married Isabella Hardie, thus combining the two earliest families in the area. Isabella's elder sister, Margaret, married Gus Topp, who came to Ellinbank with his brother, John, in 1880.

Another settler, William Pascoe, was born in Lincoln and went to New Zealand before he finally settled near Warragul in 1876. William John Dalgleish was born in North America and came to Warragul South in about 1875. David Smith was another settler whose community spirit was typical of many of the men who cleared the forest to make way for the future. People who lead hard lives usually seem more willing to share themselves and the fruits of their labours than others, for some reason. Smith donated some land to the Education Department for the school and later gave more land for the Warragul South Church. Born in Wales, he became the first Councillor for Warragul South.

There are other names of equal note, but many have gone from the district now. Only John Cropley still farms land that has been in his family since it was first selected.

It would be easy now to think that dairying has always been the main source of employment in the area but nothing could be further from the truth. Remember that this whole district was once covered by a dense forest which boasted some of the largest trees the world has ever seen. The first form of employment was, quite logically, clearing the land. In 1887, Cropleys built the Gainsborough Mill and ran eleven kilometres of tramway straight into Darnum Railway Station. They even imported their own locomotive. The Cropley tramline also carried the timber from other mills in the area. One tree the sawmillers discovered has come to be known as the 'Thorpdale

Tree'. This was measured at over 114 metres! Over 1,000 tonnes of timber per month left the Darnum Railway Station.

The grandstand at the Warragul racecourse was built, from this timber, supplied free of charge by William Smith, a member of the old Warragul Racing Club. The West Gippsland Hospital also owes its beginning to the milling industry, but for a different and more bizarre reason. The rate of injury in the mills was such that a local hospital was a necessity. Sawmilling is a dangerous trade.

Roads were always a problem in Gippsland and nowhere more so than in the hills of the Strzelecki Range. In 1904 John Cropley wrote to the Council enclosing a letter from them dated 1884 concerning a deviation of the road near his farm. He mentioned that he thought that twenty years would have been enough for them to make up their minds and that something should now be done about it. To overcome one road building problem, at one point during the construction of the main road south of Warragul an aerial tramway was used to move stone across the deep gullies to the roadworks.

Few people realise that the Country Roads Board virtually began in Warragul, or that the memorial at the junction of the Princes Highway and Lardners Track is to the honour of Calder, moving spirit of the CRB.

Very briefly, the following are some of the dates that are of significance in the history of the Ellinbank community. The first school was opened in 1879. In 1880 it was moved to its present site and the South Warragul Hotel was opened. The first wedding was on Christmas Eve 1881, in the new non-denominational church. It is a fitting footnote that the last person buried from this church was Mrs Bertha Heywood, daughter of W. T. Cropley and Fanny Smith, the couple who chose Christmas Eve 1881 to make their vows.

1885 saw the first Warragul Show. In 1888 Nestor's butter factory was opened at Bull Swamp, perhaps the first butter factory in the State. 1898 was the year of the great bushfires which swept the whole area.

Mount Worth, its slopes cleared of timber, saw the swamps and steep gullies become first-class grazing land and the hopes of the pioneers become reality. Now Mount Worth serves more often as a symbol of homecoming than of aspiration.

22 Ruby's Johann Matthies

When Johann Gottlob Matthies was naturalised on 12 January 1900, he was naturalised as a Victorian, for the Federation of Australia was not yet official. The *Letters of Naturalisation Under the Provisions of an Act of the Parliament of Victoria. No. 1063* were signed by the Right Honourable Thomas, Baron Brassey, K.C.B., Governor of Victoria and its dependencies.

Johann was the son of a citizen of Meltendorf, East Saxony, now part of the East German Peoples Republic. His mother was Renate Doening or Doering — the names on the marriage certificate are now very hard to make out. He was in Australia by the time he reached his mid-twenties. We know that he was twenty-seven when he married Polly Fidge, probably in 1886. The wedding was celebrated in the Fidge's farmhouse at Ruby, where Johann had selected land for himself. The Fidge family owned the land opposite Johann's selection and romance soon blossomed between Polly and the young German.

Times were hard for the young couple as they struggled to make the selection, named 'Glentrees', profitable. The coming of the Great Southern Railway enabled them to make a few extra shillings selling vegetables, milk, cream, butter and cheese to the railway workers.

The commercial experience he gained here led him to open a store at Ruby. The store was built in 1891 with the help of Peter Pershang, a bush carpenter. Peter's name appears in many places in South Gippsland as an itinerant carpenter.

Some time after the store was built one of Johann's bitches crawled underneath to have her pups, and one of the sons, young Ernst, was sent under the store to drag them out. There he found that the bitch had unearthed two unopened quart bottles of whisky. Johann denied all knowledge of them and assured his wife that the carpenter must have left them there. (Would you bury and then forget two quart bottles of whisky?) Whatever the truth, the bottles disappeared quietly and young Ernst was not thanked for finding them.

As with most families in those days, there were many children. The first was Mary Renate, born on 27 November 1887. The next November saw the arrival of Johann Gustav and the November after that was enlivened by the birth of Johann Ernst. Johann Oskar started a string of October births in the next year, 1890. October 1891 was the month in which Johann Herbert arrived and Johann Thomas arrived in the same month of the following year. There were no young Matthies in 1893 and perhaps that is why Mary Alice came earlier in 1894 than usual. She was born in April and Mary Mabel was born in March 1896.

In May 1900, Johann Gottlob Matthies left the store to run a farm at Nerrena. Sadly, he became very ill and only stayed on the farm a few weeks before going to Bendigo, where he died. This tragedy left his young widow in dire straits. She had eight young children to keep on a farm which was barely developed. To make matters even worse, feed for stock was very scarce that year. Butter prices were also very low and the money she earnt from cream sales was almost the only income she had.

Fortunately for Polly Matthies, and for all the other struggling farmers in the area, a butter factory was opened in Ruby which, though butter prices stayed low, at least meant some form of fairly secure income. Wood, Dunn and Company built the factory in 1896-97 and it operated from then until 1905.

The Matthies family answered the call to arms in 1914-15. Johann Oskar, Johann Herbert and Johann Thomas each enlisted to fight in the First World War. Oskar made the supreme sacrifice on the rugged hills of Gallipoli.

On a happier note, Erle Matthies, a son of Johann Ernst, showed me two of the ledgers from the old store and I copied one of the pages for interest. It includes such entries as 'Horse Shoeing ... 3s' and a 'dog-tax' of 5s. The bank with which the store dealt was the Bank of Australasia. There is reference to buying timber for a culvert for 7s 6d and to paying 'George' £2 to build a culvert. There is an entry reading 'Brown. The Southern Mail', which is a reference to a newspaper long gone; another entry records the payment of £1 10s to C. Rooney for signwriting.

There are still many relatives of Johann Gottlob Matthies living in the hill country of South Gippsland and his part in establishing the small community of Ruby will not soon be forgotten. Ruby itself has suffered something of a decline. The South Gippsland Highway now passes to the south of the town instead of through it and few of the tourists heading down from Melbourne to Wilsons Promontory or the southern beaches even realise the town exists.

23 Korumburra Coal Rush

Some settlers fought their way across the tangled ridges from Drouin. Others fought their way up along McDonalds Track from Lang Lang. From whichever direction settlers moved into the Korumburra area, they had to fight their way through dense forests, unmapped swamps and a maze of steep ridges. Some of this is mirrored in the Coal Creek Historical Park now opened at Korumburra, marking the completion of the struggle of the pioneers.

What was once a silent forest, giant gums and matted undergrowth is now a quietly prosperous shire headquarters, an established town with a wide range of amenities and a comfortable life-style. The Korumburra of today is a far cry from the 'Wild Cattle Run'. This aptly-named run extended from the Powlett River to the Tarwin and from the Strzelecki Ranges to the sea. The vast holding was named after the cattle which were abandoned when the Corinella (Red Point) convict settlement was closed in 1828. The run provided an outpost from which settlers could strike into the hills in search of land they could call their own.

In the decade following the gold rushes there were many men moving further out in search of land. The 1869 and 1878 Land Acts served as a further impetus to this movement. By 1888 most of the land in the Korumburra area was taken up. Many of the settlers came down from Drouin and gave rise to the term 'down-southers'. Others came east from the Lang Lang area which was rapidly filling up.

Among the real heroes of this trek were the surveyors sent by the Government to mark tracks and establish maps. Two of the best-known were Lardner and Whitelaw. These men often suffered great hardship. Whitelaw and his party nearly starved while cutting a track from Foster to Korumburra and Poowong. In those days Foster was called Stockyard Creek and Korumburra was still unnamed.

When the railway came through in June 1891, there was still only an embryo township. The terminus of the line was, for a time, about four kilometres west of the present Korumburra station. This point was called Whitelaw, or Whitelaws Track, after the surveyor. With the railway making access much easier and the continued influx of settlers Korumburra continued to grow slowly.

It was coal that really brought Korumburra to life.

James Brown was probably the first to find coal at Korumburra. He is reported to have found a seam in what is now Coal Creek in 1872. He, like Whitelaw, almost starved to death while trying to cross the ranges from Stockyard Creek to Bunyip. His discovery must have created some interest because surveyor R. A. F. Murray visited the site in 1873. A block of Korumburra coal was displayed in Melbourne in the mid-1880s and this caused the rapid formation of at least three mining companies. These were the Jumbunna Coal Company, The Strzelecki Coal Mine Company and the Korumburra Coal Company. All the capital raised by these companies was spent in development and they all failed soon afterwards.

The Coal Creek Proprietary Company, formed in 1889, was the first effective effort to mine Korumburra coal. Apparently the founder of the company had battled for six years to raise the necessary finance.

Soon the railway was important to the whole State as a source of coal. In 1892 a siding was opened to Coal Creek and great jubilation greeted the first train out of Korumburra loaded with local coal. This was on 28 October 1892. In 1894 a branch line was opened to the Jumbunna mines, and in 1896 this was extended to Outtrim. In 1894 a spur was also opened to the Strzelecki siding. During this period there were up to nine coal trains a day leaving Korumburra. This was at a time when the Coal Creek Proprietary Company was contracting to supply coal to the Victorian Government, having proven the superior quality of local coal.

The locomotive R 303 and her driver, T. Griffiths, had been heroes as that first heavily-decorated trainload of coal pulled out on 28 October. By the end of the year, they were just another part of busy railway teams.

It was soon found that the steep grades out of Korumburra were too much for most locomotives pulling full-length coal trains. The system was then changed. Small trains left Korumburra nine times daily for Nyora. Here, three of the smaller trains would be combined to make one large train for the trip to Dandenong and Melbourne.

John Lardner surveyed the township of Korumburra in 1887. The first sale of township allotments was held in Melbourne at the auction rooms of Munro and Baillieu on 20 January 1888. A second sale was held a few days later. Many of the buyers were genuine businessmen hoping to establish businesses in Korumburra, but there were also many speculators. The blocks were not cheap. The first sold (probably the present Shire Hall site) fetched £240. A Shire Hall was soon a necessity because local residents, confident that Korumburra would soon become the capital of the south, petitioned the Government for severance.

Their petition, seeking severance from the Shire of Buln Buln, appeared in the *Government Gazette* for December 1889. It was suggested that the new municipality should be known as the Shire of Poowong and Jeetho. The petition was unsuccessful but the local residents pursued the matter with grim determination and they were finally successful in May 1891.

The usual sign of permanence in such communities is the establishment of a school. The Korumburra school was opened as a part-time school on 27 January 1891. Children attended in the afternoons only.

The people of Korumburra seem to have had from the start a determination to improve their town as quickly as possible, most improvements being locally organised and carried out, often with only minimal help from the Government. The Coal Creek Historical Park is a fitting continuation of that attitude.

24 The Last of the Aborigines

The Kulin Aborigines, tall and vigorous, handsome and strong, were generally peaceful men. Inter-tribal wars were rare; the murder of white men was uncommon. But when trouble came to them, the

Kulin warriors could be fierce and bloodthirsty. They practiced cannibalism and sometimes dismembered living victims.

All the West Gippsland Aborigines belonged to the Kulin group of tribes. There were three main divisions of the Kulins in what we now call West Gippsland. One tribe, the Bonkoolawool, disappeared before much was known about them. Even their disappearance is a mystery. They lived in the southern part of the province and possessed the land between Cape Liptrap and Wonthaggi. American and British sealers stole Bonkoolawool women and killed many of their men in raiding parties ashore. It was possibly a smallpox epidemic, caught from the sealers, that ended the Bonkoolawool. It is not a time to remember with pride.

In the Dandenongs were the Wurundjery-balook, a sub-tribe of the Woiwurung, the tribe usually known as the Yarra tribe. The Mornington Peninsula and the area west of the Great Swamp were inhabited by the Bunurong tribes, of which there were three sub-tribes. Of these, the Yalukit-wilam lived along the shores of the Bay from Werribee to Seaford. The Narug-wilam inhabited the foothills of the Dandenong Ranges, while the Bulug-wilam lived west of the swamp and on the Peninsula.

All these tribes lived together in harmony. Monbulk was, in fact, a sanctuary area where the leaders of the various groups could meet in peace to discuss problems and settle them amicably. The Kulin rarely fought among themselves but their attacks on the tribes of the Ganai group were fierce and merciless. The Ganai, regarded as an inferior people, lived in the Central Gippsland area, east of a line drawn from Moe to Cape Liptrap.

Wives were often stolen from the Ganai and the reprisal raids were bloody affairs. About 1820 a Bunurong group on French Island was destroyed by a raiding party of Ganai, and in the early 1830s another Bunurong group was massacred in a dawn raid through the mists and marshes of Tooradin.

In February 1840, a gentleman named Clow wrote this of a 'revenge' raid by the Bunurong:

About mid-day they surprised the [Ganai] camp, making prisoners of all in it, which consisted only of some old men and some children. They then went in search of the able-bodied men, whom they espied very busily engaged in 'fishing on the banks of a large river not far off.They managed to sneak up on them, within ten or twenty yeards, and then blazed into them, killing or wounding every one of them, seven in number. Those who escaped the first volley jumped into the river and swam across, but the second volley brought them all down.

'After cutting out their kidney fat, they took as much of the carcases as they could well carry on their return route, and having mustered their forces at the camp where they had captured the old men and children, they dispatched them also, and then commenced their retreat. When they reached the first station on the Westernport side of the mountains they still had portions of the legs and thighs of their enemies, which they had not consumed, but reserved for those of the tribe who were not present.'

Many other raids took place, of course. In October 1843, twenty-four Kulin warriors killed nine men of the Ganai and brought their bodies home to be eaten. One white station-owner was offered part of the stomach fat of one victim. He declined the honour.

Kidney fat was the real prize, however.

'The part of the human body valued most by them is the kidney fat, to which they attribute supernatural powers and think it acts as a charm in many cases ... the disgusting and cruel act of cutting out the fat is very often performed while life is still lingering in the victims; several instances have occurred where they have been found alive hours after having suffered from this horrid deed.'

By 1850, warfare between the Kulin and the Ganai was over. The Ganai were now fighting for their lives against the white settlers . In the 1850s whole sub-tribes disappeared from South and Central Gippsland. In one massacre at Warrigal Creek in 1842, there were about one hundred Aborigines camped around a waterhole. White settlers surrounded them and systematically murdered every man, woman and child. There had been a number of minor attacks on whites by the Aborigines but these rarely involved killing, as usually the blacks were content to steal. These were not great crimes to put against the extermination of an entire people.

We have little to be proud of in our treatment of the Gippsland Aborigines. Those we did not kill by direct violence died from our imported diseases and from, loss of heart as their tribes and lands disappeared. The Kulins were generally fairly co-operative towards the white invaders. They might have been just as well advised to fight them from the outset.

25 The Mayor of Narre Warren

Some people have called Pat Sweeney the unofficial 'Mayor of Narre Warren'. Some have called him other names. Pat is many things but he is, above all else, a Sweeney. The toughness and courage of the mental outlook shown by the pioneer Sweeneys is Pat's proudest possession. At the drop of a snap-brim hat he will launch into an account of what those early ancestors did for, and to, the Narre Warren area.

About 1857, when the gold rushes were still going strongly, young Daniel Sweeney left Fermoy, in County Cork, Ireland, outward bound for Port Phillip and then Ballarat. Two years later his brother John came to Melbourne. John put an advertisement in a Melbourne newspaper to say he had arrived. Daniel saw the advertisement, bought a horse and rode to Melbourne. He found his brother and they bought a second horse. One way or another, the Sweeneys have been dealing in horses ever since.

As the goldfields had failed to provide Daniel with the fortune he sought, the two young Irishmen decided to try their luck on the land. They rode into Gippsland and selected land between Narre Warren and Berwick. Several generations later, during the land boom of the early 1970s, that land turned into a goldmine of a different type.

The land they selected had belonged to a Mr Watson, who was selling out to return to England. He was heartbroken at the death of his wife and baby, and wanted no more of this strange, new land. The graves of his family are still on 'Fermoy', the name the Sweeneys gave the land that reminded them so much of home.

John Sweeney soon married Miss Alice Reedy, daughter of another great pioneering family in the area. Daniel was something of a reprobate. He never married, spending his life instead in pursuit of a number of colourful entertainments involving bottles and racehorses.

He had a number of good horses at different times, including one winner, of sorts, at Beaconsfield. The course there was on the flat land behind the Central Hotel. Unfortunately, Protestants and Catholics in the young colony did not always see things eye-to-eye. The Protestant judge at Beaconsfield was not about to award a close finish to a horse owned by a man called Daniel Sweeney and with an Irish accent to boot. Unwisely, he said so in the hearing of the Irishman concerned.

There was no photo finish in those days so Daniel lodged his 'protest' in the form of a punch thrown at the judge. When the ensuing melee was broken up it was decided to call the race a 'no race'. Daniel swore to his dying day that his horse had won by 'a good head'.

He won another race on the Eummemmerring racecourse (which was where the Prince Mark Hotel stands now, on the Princes Highway in Doveton). The prize was a good saddle, worth real money to the young horseman, so he hid it very carefully before adjourning to the Hallam wine saloon. After the celebrations it was all he could do, with help, to find his horse, let alone the saddle. He came back and located it the next day.

'Fermoy' was like most other farms in the district. It was almost self-supporting and everybody was expected to work. There was a dairy herd and there were pigs. Vegetables were grown for sale and there were annual oat crops. Butter and cheese were made for sale around South Yarra and Richmond. Taking the pigs to Dandenong's Tuesday market was a major task. John Sweeney's sons would leave on Sunday, moving the pigs along on foot. This was a very slow process but, after the sale and with pockets full of money, the boys made very good time on the trip home.

They went to school at Berwick, though the younger ones were able to attend the new school opened in Narre Warren in 1889. The Hanley children, friends of the Sweeneys, walked each morning from the corner of Pound and Cranbourne Roads to 'Fermoy'. There the Sweeney kids would meet them and the little band would troop off to Berwick.

South of Narre Warren there was a large swamp. Those children who lived south of the swamp would ride to the southern edge and then hobble their horses. After wading barefoot through the swamp they would put their shoes back on and 'leg it' the rest of the way.

The Sweeneys all worshiped at St Michael's Church in Berwick. Pat remembers, as a little boy, the day the key was forgotten. Pat Curran, 'the king of stackbuilders', opened the door with a hefty kick from his very large boot. Nothing so minor as a key was going to stand in the way of Sunday worship!

The famous Andy O'Keefe was related to the Sweeneys. He was the contractor who built the Great Southern Railway between Korumburra and Tooradin. Paid £7,000 per mile, he faced and overcame many obstacles. At one point he had to build three bridges in one and a half kilometres to cross and re-cross the meandering Tarwin River. Two were 152 metres long and the other was 305 metres long.

The Sweeneys are nearly all buried in the Berwick Cemetery. I would like to think that on Monday, 1 October 1973, when Sir Rohan Delacombe proclaimed Berwick a city, some of his words might have drifted on the wind to that cemetery, only a few hundred metres from where he stood. He spoke of the efforts of the pioneering families and the sound basis they had laid for the continuing prosperity of the region.

Pat Sweeney lives at 'Florenceville', Narre Warren. It faces across the highway to the Civic Centre No. 1 Estate, once the Stuart Estate and formerly owned by the Sweeneys. On that estate there were three little boys growing up. They were Jason, Seamus and Paddy Hill, the fifth generation descendants of John and Alice Sweeney.

Pat revels in his reputation for forthrightness. He says that he has shoulders broad enough for any criticism and I think he has. Whatever his critics say, however, they can never say the Sweeneys have not played their part in our history and played it well and fairly.

Top left: Mr J. Denholm, Headmaster of Yannathan Primary School (see Story 20).
Top right: Mr W. Calder, father of the CRB. (see Story 21). Photo: Country Roads Board,
Victoria. Bottom: Something of a landmark at Wonthaggi (see Story 19)

Top: A great day for Korumburra (see Story 23).
Bottom: A sample of Korumburra mud—outside the Austral Hotel, about 1913
(see Story 23). Photo: Country Roads Board, Victoria

26 For Whom the School Bell Tolls

In 1872 the Victorian Parliament passed the historic Education Act. For the first time schooling was compulsory and tuition was free. Now the State of Victoria has celebrated the centenary of the opening of the first free schools. A film was made and books were written; each school compiled a small history.

These notes are from the history of Primary School No. 3033, Beaconsfield. This school has had its share of colourful moments over the years. Not yet a hundred years old, but is not far short of it either, the title transfer for the school property is dated 8 October 1889 and the school was opened in 1890. This makes it something of a youngster among the other schools in the district. What is now the Berwick Primary School was going strong in 1876; Narre Warren North's school was opened in 1872 and Harkaway took in its first pupils in 1880.

Until 1890 the children of Beaconsfield who desired an education attended classes in a private house at the corner of Manuka Road and the Gippsland Road, now the Princes Highway. The fee was one shilling per week, a significant sum in those days. The first classroom built at Beaconsfield was just over seven metres by five and a half metres, small by the standards of today. In 1890 it was expected to house fifty children where, in 1974, thirty seem to fill the room. Average attendance was only thirty-three however, so they must have fitted in at least that number.

It was a solidly-constructed room — so sturdy, in fact, that it is in better repair than the rooms built later and is still in regular use — and it was used for a wide variety of purposes. From 1891 it was used for Sunday School and religious services. In 1895 permission was granted for its use for a 'Magic Lantern Entertainment', the rental to be 'under the usual conditions — 2 shillings and sixpence'.

I don't know why Beaconsfield Railway Station State School was built so long after the Berwick school. Licensing Court figures quoted in Early Days of Berwick show that in 1890 there were 2190 people in Beaconsfield and only 1050 in Berwick. Perhaps the people of Berwick were better at dealing with politicians. More probably, the fact that Beaconsfield's population contained a fair number of goldminers and timbercutters meant that the residents were more interested in hotels than in schools.

The facts seem to bear this out. The Gippsland Hotel (Bowman's Inn) was apparently operating well before 1860. It is now the Central Hotel. The Cardinia Park Hotel (originally the Bush Inn) was operating by 1890, when the school was built, and there were two hotels in Upper Beaconsfield (the Pine Grove Hotel and Beaconsfield House). As well, a 'Colonial Wine Licence' was taken out in the name of James Kirwin or Kirwan.

The name Beaconsfield Railway Station State School was changed late in 1890 to Lower Beaconsfield State School. It was later changed again but, no doubt, the growing holiday resort of Upper Beaconsfield felt much better for having a Lower Beaconsfield.

Patrick Lohan was the first Headmaster. He arrived when the school was opened and left in 1895 when the enrolment dropped. This has been a recurring problem for the school, which has not long had more than one hundred pupils. The Lohans had four children when they arrived in Beaconsfield and twins were born while they were there. A special school holiday was declared to celebrate the happy event! Those were the good old days.

Unfortunately, when Mr Lohan left he took the school keys with him. A window was forced open and this served as an entrance for both teacher and pupils until the keys were returned. There was also a dispute over the toilets, or 'out offices' as the Education Department called them. An outgoing teacher refused to empty them and the incoming teacher said that it wasn't his responsibility to empty pans that had been filled during the appointment of the previous teacher. They stayed unemptied for a long time. Even in those days, teachers were expected to do a great deal more than teach.

From March 1895, to March 1902, the school came under the control of Henry G. Rankine, Headmaster at Berwick. He attended Beaconsfield on one day each week to supervise the instruction given by the pupil-teacher. Grades I, II and III were conducted at Beaconsfield by the pupil-teacher while Grades IV, V and VI walked to Berwick each day.

Joseph Morgan was Headmaster from 1902 to 1908. He travelled each day from Pakenham, a fair ride in those days. Morgan tried to do what is now common policy — he tried to make the school part of the community. He formed a cadet corps and he held many picnics, excursions and field days in which the adults of the town were encouraged to participate.

The 'School Committee Records' show a few matters of interest. In May 1920, a letter was written to the Education Department respectfully pointing out that the desks promised for 1915 had not yet arrived! An unusual request is also included in the records. Should anyone know the whereabouts of Roland Hill, born in July 1918, or his sister, Myrtle, born in September 1919, the school, it is said, would appreciate hearing from them. School records show their destination on leaving the school as 'unknown'. Until it is known to which school they went, it is impossible to complete their transfer and they cannot continue their education!

The old schoolroom was decorated in the usual style. One local resident who had attended the school before the Second World War came back as a fireman to help teachers plan a fire drill. He said, 'Yes, this is the room I was in. Hasn't changed much, either, except for the pictures. We had Burke and Wills being speared to death on one wall and Lasseter dying of thirst on the other. Leichhardt was being speared to death near the door and Queen Victoria hung at the back there disapproving of the whole thing. She was a cheerful old room, all right!'

Times change and so do communities. Beaconsfield is now a dormitory town and no longer a rural hamlet where everyone knows everyone else. The school's role has changed from that of a social centre to solely that of an educational facility. Perhaps the Education Department's policy of community involvement in schools may give Beaconsfield a new centre where the community can again become cohesive. Who knows?

27 Mountain Men from Hill End

Surveyors before the turn of the century were hardy fellows. They had to be. They spent months at a time in primitive areas, in dense scrub, swamps and the ranges of the Great Divide. They were also constantly frustrated by the refusal of settlers to pay any attention to the results of their work. The 'mountain men' of the Hill End, Tangil and Willow Grove areas were like most settlers. They built their tracks where the ground was driest and their towns followed the tracks. Maps were all very well, but a map wouldn't keep a bullock-team out of a bog.

Hill End, like Topsy, just 'grow'd'.

Pearson and Reoch had a cattle run in the area by 1850. Three men took up blocks following the Land Act of 1869; they were Charles Gadd, J. Varney and J. Hasthorpe. Gadd was already living in the Hill End area and running a small store at the time.

Apparently the usual practice was to find a good spot, set up house, clear it, plant a crop and, when there was time, apply for a survey. The survey made the whole thing legal but no-one seemed to bother too much about sticking to the lines on the map. This must have broken the hearts of the 'perfectionist and straight-line' surveyors like Lardner.

Hector Lamont was another early settler at Hill End. He came from the Western District to join his cousin, Farquhar Morrison. Hector was a builder and built a weatherboard house with an iron roof, which was widely regarded at the time as rather a 'grand' structure. Their next house went one better, though. It was built for Hector's brother by Larry Cummin, a miner at Russells Creek. It had Baltic pine boards, an Oregon frame, an iron roof and even a swing-arm in the fireplace for pots, kettles and camp-ovens. And not only did it have all these grand features; it was painted! Most people saw it as the first 'proper' house in the district. This was about 1866.

The first school was built after 1866, of slabs with a shingle roof, and the first teacher was Miss Louisa Westoby. She didn't last long as a 'Miss'. Tom Irvine saw his opportunity for matrimony and took it. Any young woman who wanted a husband in those days had only to become a teacher in a small country school. Single women were always scarce in what was still largely a 'frontier country'. (The same thing still applies, to some extent!)

The first settler at Willow Grove (apart from the many transient miners) was probably the same Tom Irvine, or his father. Tom and his wife set up a restaurant on the Melbourne to Sale road in 1866. In 1867 the Tangil Track joined the road nearby.

The story of Thomas Needham was typical of that of many early settlers. He made the six-month trip from England with his wife and five children, one of the children dying on the trip out. The family went at first to Bet Bet, near Ballarat, where they made a living selling oaten chaff to the miners. Later they followed the miners into Gippsland and decided on Willow Grove almost by accident.

The selection Needham took up was on the north bank of the Latrobe River where the family existed by raising vegetables, oats, fruit and sheep. The trip to Melbourne for supplies took three weeks and was made once every six months. Later, Mrs Needham was able to buy supplies in Walhalla. Soon the Needhams were supplying not only the miners and prospectors in the hills, but also the railway workers between Drouin and Moe. At that time, Moe was just a small trackside encampment.

Thomas Needham died in 1890 but his life's work was completed. He had seen his children take up land in the district and there are still Needhams on the land there.

There were good times and bad times still in store for the farmers at Willow Grove. In 1892 a creamery was opened and the farmers had a new market. In 1905 it closed down because many farmers had bought their own separators, but in that year the draining of the Trafalgar Swamp was completed. The farmers along the Latrobe cut a track towards Trafalgar and sent their cream to the factory there.

In 1912 the ubiquitous rabbit appeared and spread rapidly, and for the next decade farmers fought a losing baffle; it was not until myxomatosis was introduced in 1949 that the menace eased. A drought year occurred in 1914 and sheep were sent into Gippsland from most other parts of Victoria. Even so, losses were staggering.

The years of the First World War brought even greater sadness as men from these small farming communities answered the call to duty. The names carved on memorials do nothing to assuage the sorrow of those left behind.

In 1934 Gippsland saw its worst-ever floods. These were, strangely enough, very late in the year. There was no loss of human life but stock losses were high. After the flood, farmers had a scant five years to re-establish themselves before the disaster of the 1939 bushfires. Again, there was no loss of life in the Willow Grove area but the economic damage was grave indeed.

The Fumina settlement was a late developer. It was surveyed by
D. M. Boyd in 1890 and the following ten years saw a steady influx
of settlers, so that by 1900 there were twenty-six children of school
age in the township. A paling school was erected and Miss Ada
Gill was transferred from Geelong. I don't know whether she was
snapped-up by some bachelor or not, but Miss Mary Quinlan was
in charge of the rebuilt school in 1904.

The names that were known to the farmers and the miners of the
past have in many cases gone and been forgotten. Russells Creek,
Wombat Creek and Hawthorne Creek were well-known names
which are remembered by only a few. Tangil has become Tanjil and
even Gippslanders usually have only a hazy idea of the locations of
the towns of Hill End, Willow Grove and Fumina.

28 Coaches, Coal and Natural Gas—
The Gippsland Corridor

Berwick Hill was a thirsty place a hundred years ago. Cobb and
Co coaches struggled up it and rattled down the other side to
change horses and quaff a few quick ales at Souters Hotel (now the
Central Hotel) at Beaconsfield. The route the coaches followed into
Gippsland has now become a part of the Gippsland Corridor, part
of the Great Valley of Victoria.

For more than one hundred years, Gippsland has supplied
Melbourne with food through the Corridor. Today water, food,
power and labour all pass down it into the metropolitan area. The
Corridor runs east from Dandenong along the foothills of the ranges,
skirts what was once the Great Swamp, climbs over the old volcanic
ridge between Drouin and Warragul and then drops into the Latrobe
Valley. It is hemmed in by the Great Dividing Range to the north
and the Strzeleckis to the south. The backbone of the Corridor is the
Princes Highway. If the Corridor were to close, perhaps in time of
war, it would be almost impossible for Melbourne to survive.

The Princes Highway has grown from a barely passable track in
the 1850s, only wide enough for a man on horseback, to one of the

nation's busiest roads. A coach trip along the Gippsland Road, or the Old Sale Road, was an adventure. In summer the coach was scheduled to reach Sale from Melbourne in just twenty-two hours. In winter, this became twenty-seven hours and the coach was rarely on time even then. Departure was usually from the Albion Hotel in Bourke Street; coaches left from this point for the hills of Gippsland, the grassy plains of the west and the busy goldfields to the north.

The Gippsland route lay along what is now Dandenong Road and followed what is now the Princes Highway to about Garfield North. There the route became a little flexible, depending on conditions. Some coaches went well north of the Gippsland Road and followed the Old Telegraph Road through Jindivick. Then they picked up the Old Sale Road, which left the present route of the Princes Highway at what was once called Whisky Creek, and joined it again east of Trafalgar.

Horses were changed at Oakleigh and again at Dandenong. Then came the 'pause that refreshes' at Souter's at Beaconsfield where the horses were changed again. This hotel and the Cardinia Park Hotel, a little to the north and formerly called the Bush Inn, were built on the two most popular crossings of the Cardinia Creek. The next change of horses was at Pakenham, followed by Buneep (now Bunyip, but actually somewhat to the north of the present township) and the Robin Hood Hotel.

Fresh horses were harnessed at Brandy Creek and then at Shady Creek, north of Darnum. Moe, Morwell, Traralgon, Rosedale and Kilmany were other staging points before the coaches reached Sale. Con Hildebrand is believed to have been the first driver to have take a coach through to Sale, taking three days to get there. Con died just a few months before the first aeroplane landed at Sale.

Of all the Victorian districts, Gippsland had the worst and the most frequently impassable roads. Now it has a major highway with a second loop from Dandenong to Sale by way of the south coast. The coming of the railway is described elsewhere in these pages. By the turn of the century, the Corridor contained rail and road networks but it took many years more to build up the complex of feeder and access roads and branch lines, some now closed for economic reasons.

In 1866 J. Cosmo Newbery discovered large deposits of brown coal in the Latrobe Valley. Various companies were formed to mine the coal, including the Great Morwell Coal Mining Company, which took up a lease in 1887. On 25 September 1917, a committee reporting to Parliament suggested the setting-up of the State Electricity Commission. Another great invasion of Gippsland was about to take place.

On 24 June 1924, Gippsland began exporting electricity to Melbourne, down the Corridor, for the first time. At first, the four circuits from Yallourn carried 132,000 volts each. Later, 220,000-volt circuits were added and, finally, 500,000-volt circuits. Each of these up-gradings was a pioneer step in the transmission of bulk electricity. Australia generally, and Victoria particularly, have led the world in this field. But electricity was not the only power export.

Briquettes were made at the Great Morwell Open Cut Mine about 1892, but they could not compete with black coal prices and production stopped. Now briquettes, a major industrial and domestic power source, flow endlessly down the Corridor to Melbourne.

Oil exploration in Bass Strait led to the next major development of the Corridor. Natural gas fields have been developed as a valuable consequence of this oil exploration, and are a major national asset. Soon this great power source was flowing down the Gippsland Corridor.

In August 1967, the Victorian Pipelines Commission received tenders for the construction of a pipeline from Dutson, near Sale, to Dandenong. The pipeline was to bring natural gas to Melbourne. This required the supplying and laying of 178 kilometres of pipe seventy-six centimetres in diameter, some of it especially strengthened for laying under roads, rivers, railways and proposed urban developments.

Water is vital to a city, of course, and water is one more Gippsland export, so much so that some Gippslanders are now suffering shortages. As the urban sprawl spread down over the Mornington Peninsula engineers again looked to the east for salvation. First came the damming of Haunted Gully at Beaconsfield and the transferring into it of water from the Toomuc Creek by open channel. This was to supply the Flinders Naval Base, beginning in 1916.

In 1925-26 water was diverted from the Upper Bunyip River. After the Second World War, water was also taken from the Tarago River. Now there is a large dam on the Tarago, feeding the

Beaconsfield and Lysterfield reservoirs. The process was continued with the Moondarra Dam and later the Thompson River scheme.

The Corridor is no historical accident. Through a narrow strip, only a few kilometres wide, comes what is literally the life-blood of Melbourne. With the Corridor closed, Melbourne could not survive.

29 Sir John Monash—Giver of Power to the People

Sir John Monash was a great man. Most people realise that and accept it, but few realise just how much Victoria owes him. His drive, energy and skill ensured his possession of the title 'Father of the State Electricity Commission', yet he is much better known for his military skill.

Louis Monash arrived in Australia in 1853, aged twenty-one years. He married soon after and on 23 June 1865, in a terrace house in Dudley Street, West Melbourne, his son, John, was born. John's first school was St Stephen's School in Richmond but his parents moved to Jerilderie soon after. There he learnt to ride and to shoot. His intellectual ability was so obvious that his school-master at Jerilderie, Bill Elliot, spent many hours teaching the boy things beyond the normal curriculum. He urged the Monash family to take John back to Melbourne where he could get better schooling.

In 1877, John Monash entered Scotch College. By 1881 he was equal dux of the school. He entered Melbourne University to study Civil Engineering at the age of sixteen, coaching other students to raise money for his books and fees. In 1884 he had to leave the University for financial reasons. He was fortunate in securing a position with the firm building the Princes Bridge over the Yarra, where he was given charge of all the earthworks and masonry. The firm (David Munro and Company) then gave him further experience on other bridges around Melbourne. Early in 1887, aged only twenty-two, John Monash was put in charge of the construction of the Outer Circle Railway from Fairfield Park to Oakleigh. At the same time he completed his degree in Civil Engineering.

In 1891 he married Victoria, daughter of the early colonist, Moton Moss. Monash obtained his Masters Degree in Civil Engineering in 1893 and two years later qualified in Law. He said that he felt 'it was handy for an engineer to have some idea of the law'. At about this time the great land boom collapsed and work became very hard to find. After a short period with the Harbour Trust he went into private practice as a consulting engineer.

In 1896 he designed the Anderson Street Bridge over the Yarra near the Botanic Gardens. This represented an engineering breakthrough in the use of reinforced concrete and was widely copied. He had made such a name for himself that he was asked to take command of the newly formed Victorian section of the Intelligence Corps, becoming a Lieutenant-Colonel. He had some military experience through having been a member of the militia.

When the First World War broke out he was given command of the Fourth Infantry Brigade as a Colonel. He commanded the brigade so well on Gallipoli that he was promoted to Brigadier-General. The brigade moved to France in June of 1916, and soon Monash because a Major-General, commanding the Third Division around Armentieres and at the battle for Messines.

In March 1918 the Germans broke through the Fifth Army. Monash was ordered to hold them. Somehow he got his men into position between the Ancre and the Somme, where he held the Germans and preserved the Allied defence. Monash was knighted in the field by King George V, and he became a Lieutenant-General, commanding all five Australian divisions in France. A British division, two Canadian divisions and two American divisions were added to his command at various times. He was the first British General to command American troops — and he was an Australian.

Monash organised the demobilisation of the Australian Infantry Forces and was responsible for the organisation of the Anzac Day ceremonies, including the first Anzac Day march.

In October of 1920 the Government again called on him, this time to take charge of the fledgling State Electricity Scheme, forerunner of the State Electricity Commission. As General Manager, Monash now became important to Gippslanders. In 1920 tenders for the Yallourn power house had been taken; in 1921 the first sod was turned. While the building of the power station continued a track 193 kilometres long was cut through the bush for the transmission lines. In 1924 the first electricity flowed down those long lines to the city of Melbourne.

In the meantime Monash arranged for the extension of the Newport railway power house. The increased power from this prevented a lag in the city's industrial development while Yallourn was being completed. Monash also organised the extension of the original Yallourn power station and the construction of another. The power stations along the Rubicon were also established under his control.

Sir John Monash chaired the Royal Commission into the circumstances of the police strike in 1923, and he represented the Commonwealth in a dispute over who was to control the building of Australia's two cruisers. He took a prominent part in the selection of a design and in the construction of the Shrine of Remembrance and he represented Australia at the opening of New Delhi.

Sir John Monash died on 8 October 1931. His huge State funeral was some small measure of the esteem in which his countrymen held him and a small tribute to his great contribution to the State of Victoria and to Australia.

30 Strzelecki—The Bogus Count Who Did Not Discover Gippsland

'Count' Paul Edmund De Strzelecki was a man of some mystery. Although he spent only four years in this country he was hailed as a Polish nobleman, as the discoverer of the Gippsland area and as an expert geologist. In truth, his claims to these things were very shaky indeed. Yet his name has endured where more worthy ones have not. The Range that forms the backbone of South and Central Gippsland still bears his name.

Strzelecki was born near Poznan in a part of Poland then occupied by the Russians. His parents were peasant farmers and the title of 'Count' seems to have been entirely his own idea.

His first serious love affair was with the fifteen-year-old daughter of wealthy landowners nearby. Perhaps he was really in love, but there is a suggestion that he saw the relationship with the girl, Adyna Turno, as a quick way to advance himself in the world. It seems likely that the young Strzelecki was willing to seek fame and wealth through any avenues available to him. Certainly he was very ambitious. The girl's father 'warned him to keep away' and Strzelecki apparently decided not to tempt fate. He left the district.

Later he managed the estates of Prince Sapieha. He made a considerable amount of money out of this but, when the Prince died, Strzelecki argued with the heirs. Again he left the district. In 1825 he moved to England, touring widely and learning the language. Between 1835 and 1840 he toured America and the Pacific. This gave him an interest in minerals which later served him well in Australia. He was apparently a charming fellow, and his travels seem to have cost him very little.

In 1839 he arrived in New South Wales. At this time he was a gentleman forty-two years of age, of means, claiming a noble background and able to discuss a wide range of subjects with ease and charm.

The 'Count' decided on a geological survey of the south and almost immediately found gold. The Governor, Sir George Gipps, had become a close friend and he begged Strzelecki to keep the find a secret. His journal eventually mentioned gold 'sufficient to prove its presence, insufficient to repay its extraction'. He also reported having found traces of silver.

His next trip was into the Snowy Mountains and thence to Port Phillip. McMillan had already found a way into Gippsland from the Monaro and settlement from the north and the south had already begun. Yet Strzelecki spoke of 'exploration' and seemed determined to claim all the fame for himself.

Strzelecki and James Macarthur hired two servants and an Aboriginal guide for the journey. They were joined by an Englishman, James Riley, and their journey began in high spirits in 1840. Soon after, Strzelecki climbed and named Mount Kosciusko, giving it the name of a Polish national hero. Later it was shown that the peak he climbed was not the highest after all, so the name was conveniently transferred. The party then moved down into the

Murray Valley and across the Great Dividing Range to Omeo. They were now following McMillan's tracks quite closely and making very good time.

The Tambo Valley and the Corner Inlet area were all that Strzelecki hoped they would be. He reported very favourably on them, neglecting to mention that McMillan had already been over most of the same ground. He even renamed many of the features McMillan had named. All this was in the autumn of the year. The weather was good and the party was enjoying itself, though they had forded eight deep rivers by the time they drew near Corner Inlet.

Strzelecki never actually reached Corner Inlet. The area north of the Inlet was heavily wooded and supplies were running low, so the party decided to push on for Western Port. The horses were growing weak and this was a source of concern. He would have been even more concerned had he known that the horses would soon be either abandoned or destroyed.

It was now that Strzelecki's knowledge of navigation was put to the test. His method was simple, and nearly disastrous. He simply ruled a line on the map from the point at which they stood to the shores of Western Port Bay. Any of the early settlers of Gippsland could have told him that, in the hills, the shortest distance between two points is most definitely not a straight line. He followed his compass line come hell or high water, and his party encountered plenty of both. It is true that this sort of straight-line navigation makes it unlikely that one will become lost, but it also means encountering every obstacle head-on without ever going around them. If Strzelecki's ghost ever goes exploring, I won't be volunteering to join him!

The scrub was extraordinarily dense. The rate of progress slowed dramatically. For days on end, as they crossed the Great Swamp, the explorers' feet never touched the ground as they clambered over the tangled ti-tree forest. It took fourteen days of very hard physical work before they reached the shores of Western Port. There is a persistent story that the party was helped by convicts escaped from the abandoned Corinella convict settlement, closed some twelve years before.

When the party emerged near Tooradin, their clothes were nearly torn from them by the bush. They had nearly starved, resorting to the raw flesh of koalas killed by their black guide. They were severely lacerated and bleeding. It had been impossible to light a fire in the swamp and their horses had been abandoned very early in the piece.

Strzelecki's discomfort was soon forgotten, however. His report was widely published, telling of a journey that had been a considerable feat and it did encourage settlers to press on into Gippsland. In the fuss made over Strzelecki, the work of Angus McMillan was nearly forgotten. What McMillan had called 'New Caledonia', Strzelecki called 'Gippsland', Governor Gipps having become a close friend. Other names were changed too. The 'Providence Ponds' named by McMillan became 'Perry River'.

Count Paul Edmund de Strzelecki, as he now styled himself, then went to Van Diemens Land where he carried out an extensive exploration of the interior. Then, in 1842, he explored a number of islands in Bass Strait. After returning to England, which he had adopted as his home, he published a very successful book called *Physical Descriptions of New South Wales and Van Diemen's Land*. This led to a number of people emigrating who might not otherwise have done so.

So history will record a very mixed picture of a Polish adventurer in Australia. Perhaps he was a fraud, and I am certain that he was a hunter after glory, but no-one can deny that he did a great deal of good.

31 Death-stalked Goldseeker Lewis Vieusseux

When Lewis Vieusseux took his wife and children to Australia he did not know that the country would, at first, be very cruel. Three tragedies lay in store for him.

Lewis Alexis Vieusseux was born in London on 3 March 1824. He married a Dutch girl, Julie Agnes Elizabeth Matthies, who was born at Zwalben, Holland, on 4 August 1818. Not long after the wedding, Lewis and his bride came to Victoria to look for gold. His brother went to California for the same reason, but neither of the brothers had much luck.

The first tragedy was the death of one son, Stephen Andre John Vieusseux, who lived only fifteen months and two days. The second tragedy was even more dramatic. On 2 January 1858, the Vieusseux family went into the hills near Ferntree Gully. Perhaps they were prospecting or perhaps it was a family picnic. It hardly matters what the reason was. Ferntree Gully was then a wild and lonely area of dense bush and steep hills. Little Lewis was riding a horse. The rest of the family were in a buggy. Lewis said he would ride ahead to the top of a hill and would meet the family there. He was never seen alive again.

The Vieusseux family bible has this entry in its yellowing pages:

'Lewis Stephen Arthur Vieusseux born April 29th, 1850 at 13 Rutland Street, Mornington Crescent, London. Lost in the Dandenong Ranges, Victoria, January 2nd 1858. His remains were found January 5th 1860 up in the same ranges on the bank of a small creek about 10 miles from where he was last seen. Interred in his mother's coffin in the Melbourne Cemetery, March 12th, 1878. The Lord gave and the Lord hath taken away. Blessed be the name of the Lord.'

Despite the last lines in the bible entry, Vieusseux did not readily accept the loss of his young son, only seven years old when he died. He made an extensive search himself and he enlisted the aid of the police, including a blacktracker, but the police were unable to start a search immediately.

Vieusseux apparently took them to task for this, for there is a letter dated 18 January 1858 still available which is from the Chief Commissioner of Police, explaining the delay. The letter reads:

'In reference to your letter of the 9th instant respecting the assistance required from the police at Dandenong in helping search for your son lost in the ranges I have the honour to inform you that the sergeant reports that immediately he was in a position to afford the services of the police for the purpose he procured an aboriginal tracker and carried on the search.

I very much regret that the unavoidable absence of Inspector Leech from the station and the police being required to extinguish a fire in the paddock and for other urgent duties, precluded the possibility of more prompt and unremitting search being made.

I have the honour to be, Sir, your most obedient servant,

C. MacMahon,

Chief Commissioner.'

It would be interesting to know what other 'urgent duties' were more important than the finding of a child lost in the bush. It is also interesting to note that, though the letter bears the title 'Chief Commissioner' there was no such appointment until 1880.

Another sad and distasteful note creeps in with the making of an extortion attempt upon the grieving parents. It seems there have always been people ready to see the grief of others as an opportunity to profit. The Vieusseux family received this letter on 20 August 1858:

'Mrs Vousoue,
School,
Victoria Parade,
Collingwood.

Marm did you not lose a little boy at Farn Tree Gullay abot twelve month ago well i and my mate knows all about him and if you will pay the reward i will tell you everything about him i am going to Highburghe [Heidelberg?] now but i will meet you tonight at 9 at the Post Office you and your husband come alone i wont nobody anything about him but you and your husband i wont have anything to do with a Police man but if you come alone and your husband you will get your boy i will not tell a police man and you must give i and my mate the reward i will see you at the post office my mate knows you at 9 tonight.

Your humble servant
Henry White.'

Of course, 'Henry White' and his mate never turned up. They raised the hopes of the parents and then dashed them cruelly. The reward the Vieusseux family had offered was, incidentally, £200, a huge sum in those days.

The last sad note in the short history of the little boy came on 14 January 1860. The Coroner for the District of Bourke, Samuel Curtis Caudlen, reported that he had identified the remains of Lewis Stephen Arthur Vieusseux, and ordered that the remains be buried.

Top: Steele's Hotel, Berwick, just before the first World War (see Story 25).
Photo: Country Roads Board, Victoria.
Bottom: An early view of Berwick Railway Station (see Story 28)

Top: Turning the first sod at Yallourn (see Story 29).
Bottom: An early photograph of the Yallourn open cut (see Story 29)

The third tragedy of Vieusseux's life came with the death of his beloved Julie, who died on 11 March 1878. The son who survived was Edward Vieusseux, founder of Berwick Grammar School and East Melbourne Ladies College. Some of his descendants still live in the Berwick area ... but that is another story.

32 Nellie Melba—A Legend in Her Lifetime

Dame Nellie Melba became a legend in her own lifetime, but there were many people who wondered whether she was really the heroine she seemed to be. Some saw her as a national sweetheart; some saw her as a grand ambassadress; others saw her as a scheming and calculating businesswoman, devoted to her career and unwilling to let anyone or anything stand in the way of her success.

Melba was born Helen Porter Mitchell at Burnley, near Melbourne, on 19 May 1861. Her father was David Mitchell, a Scottish migrant who had established a very successful contracting business in Melbourne. From the outset it was obvious that her voice was unusually good and her parents realised that it should be trained. At the age of three she was under the tuition of a singing-master, Signor Cecchi, who said she had a natural trill and breath control. At six she was singing in public concerts.

Her first real public appearance was at the age of ten, when she sang 'Comin' Through The Rye' at a concert in Richmond. Newspaper critics reported calmly that the young girl had a good future before her and was already quite an accomplished singer. None of them could have known that a few years later she would fill all the great concert halls of the world.

In 1882 Helen Porter Mitchell married Charles Nisbitt Frederick Armstrong, younger son of the Irish baronet, Sir Andrew Armstrong. They had one son, George, but the marriage was not a success. Her husband and her parents accompanied her to London to help launch her international career but the future she had chosen for herself left no room for husband or family. She and her husband simply drifted apart as she spent less and less time with him or with her young son. She never lost contact with her son altogether, though, and he was with her when she died. It seems, nonetheless, that she was able to spend very little time being a mother.

Armstrong bought Coombe Cottage, a picturesque home at Coldstream which Melba steadily filled with art treasures from around the world. For many years it was publicly assumed that Melba would leave all this to the nation as her memorial when she died. She never denied the assumption but it was proved to be untrue.

David Mitchell, her father, later became a wealthy farmer on a property at Lilydale, not far from Coombe Cottage. Mitchell was a hard-headed businessman who believed that a woman did not need a career of her own and that, if she decided to pursue a career, it should be something much more reliable than singing. It was many years before he was convinced that his daughter had made the right decision. Despite this, he helped her financially until she became a wealthy woman in her own right. There is a strong suggestion that she could be just as hard-headed in business matters as her father.

Melba chose her stage name to honour Melbourne, the city of her birth, but she did so only after she was certain that she could make the name famous. Her first concert in London was on 1 June 1886. It was a failure. In desperation, she went to see Madame Marchesi, perhaps the world's foremost singing-teacher. Marchesi recognised Melba's talent; she also saw that the powerful voice of the young woman needed much training and she set to work immediately.

On 12 October 1887, Mrs Armstrong, as she had been known, sang in a production of *Rigoletto* in Brussels, using the name 'Melba' for the first time. Success was immediate. On 24 May 1888, she sang the leading role in *Lucia di Lammermoor* at Covent Garden. In 1891 she received an Imperial Command to sing before the Czar Nicholas. In the six-year period from 1887 to 1893 she also drew packed houses at the Grand Opera in Paris, La Scala in Milan and in Sweden and Holland. She also sang in every Covent Garden season. Nellie Melba came back to Melbourne a national heroine. In 1892 she sang at a series of concerts in Australian cities. Everywhere she was greeted with thunderous applause and a singularly uncritical welcome.

Though she received many honours during her lifetime, the one she held most precious was that of Dame Commander of the Order of the British Empire. This award was made by King George V in recognition of her work entertaining the troops of the British Empire forces. She was always available to sing to them and it was her wish never to refuse any engagement that could help assuage the rigours of war for the men. For many years, legend has it that she received a small posy of flowers after each performance from a one-legged soldier who attended all her concerts.

Melba was involved in something of a scandal in 1928 when the biography of Clara Butt, a well-known British singer, was published. Mrs Butt claimed that she had sought Melba's advice about a repertoire for a forthcoming tour of Australia that she, the English singer, was to make. Melba was reported to have answered: 'Sing em muck! It's all they understand'. She later denied this most strongly and forced the publisher to remove the words from all the unsold copies of the biography. Even so, her reputation in Australia was somewhat damaged.

Early in 1931 newspapers carried reports that Melba was gravely ill. In banner headlines they announced on 23 February of that year that the great singer had lost her five-week fight with death. Her body was taken from St Vincent's Private Hospital at Darlinghurst to be placed aboard the 7.25 p.m. Melbourne express. At the border a Military Guard carried the coffin during the change of trains necessary at Albury. Every station along the route was crowded with bareheaded mourners.

An afternoon service at Scots Church, Melbourne, was followed by her funeral at Lilydale. The road was again lined for a large part of the way with grieving crowds.

Whatever her personal qualities, she was a great singer and the nation from which she came mourned her. After all her great overseas successes, the hills of home were here.

33 The Ure Family and 'Silver Wells'

Just over a hundred years ago, the Ure family established their homestead at 'Silver Wells'. Many people consider this to have been the original Gembrook. The Ures were a hardy and successful pioneering family and it was fitting that much of the interest in the

Gembrook centenary celebrations in 1974 centred around 'Silver Wells'. There the original log cabin built by John and Jane Ure in the summer of 1874 still stands.

When the Ures came to Australia they were a happy young couple despite the rigours of the long ocean journey. Their second son, John, was only six months old when they landed. His older brother, Alec, was two years old. Mrs Ure was the sister of the Hon. James Buchanan, M.L.C., one of the more prominent early settlers of the Berwick district. She married John Ure at Kirkintulloch, Scotland. The marriage certificate, which speaks of 'the banns having been read and there being no objection', is still in the possession of the Ure family.

The new settlers came to James Buchanan's home when they arrived in Australia in 1874. Three weeks later, John drove a bullock team into the hills north of Berwick in search of good grazing land. He found the land he sought in the new area of Gembrook, where the first settlers were beginning to take up land. The original property was of eighty-six hectares. The slopes were heavily timbered but the soil was rich and red.

The area was still remote. Pakenham was the main centre for supplies. There was also a track leading to Berwick but it took a full day each way to travel to either town.

John Ure immediately got down to work. The home he first built still stands (though only just!) and the construction is a credit to him. By autumn of 1875 there were twenty hectares cleared and sown to pasture. In May of that year he brought his young wife and his two sons to the property for the first time.

The first well sunk yielded plentiful supplies of clear, fresh water immediately. The delighted Mrs Ure promptly named the property 'Silver Wells', the name on the gate to this day.

Two more sons, Robert and James, were born at 'Silver Wells'. Perhaps because of the four boys a football ground was prepared near the house. There were other sports, too. Horse-racing, cricket, foot-racing and sheaf-tossing were popular pastimes. These were the days in which you made your own entertainment or went without.

To attend Berwick Shire Council meetings, John Ure often left home the day before and returned the day after, being away from home for three days to attend a one-day meeting.

Other settlers followed the Ures. The miners and gem-seekers were moving on further into the hills and the population was becoming more permanent. The timber industry began to grow and provided most of the employment in the district for many years. It is still an active business.

As the farm became established the group of buildings was extended. A cheese-room was added. A store and post office came next, and then a butcher's shop was attached. These represented the first commercial centre in the area. Stables and equipment sheds were built, followed by a 'smithy', a vital facility in those days.

In the butcher's shop the main chopping block is still to be seen and the iron hooks for carcases are still embedded in the thick logs of the wall. The boiler and the huge scales still stand in the cheese-room among the forms and moulds used to make cheese eighty years ago. In the store, the shelves and the counters stand. Along the shelves are the jars and bottles of a bygone age. Among the rubbish in one corner is an old box of ammunition for a rifle long since lost. Old crucibles and a retort lie gathering dust, for gold from the hills and streams around is no longer brought to 'Silver Wells' for sale. There is a rectangular hole cut in one wall for the mail, a receptacle for the written reflections of a life-style that is ended.

After 'Silver Wells' was well-established young John Ure began a farm and mill of his own out at Pancake Creek, powered by a huge water-wheel. He also owned a well-regarded bullock-team. These teams were the only way to move heavy loads through the forests and the steep hills over unmade roads. It once took young John and a friend fourteen days to transport a boiler weighing ten tonnes from the railway at Woori Yallock to Beenak. The job was worth £20. It was also at Beenak that young John found his bride. She was Rose Harrington of 'Clover Dell', a lass from Devonshire.

Jane Ure was a keen gardener. The roses, honeysuckle and jasmine she planted surround the old house and the later homes that were built nearby. The pines and the oaks she planted still stand, majestic giants guarding the place where she laboured to make a home for her family.

Jane and John Ure are long dead, but they have left their mark upon the land they came to love. The farm that was home to them is still home to the Ures, and that is as it should be.

34 Gold Fever Unlocks the Gembrook Hills

The first white men to push into the hills and dense forests between the Yarra Valley and the Great Swamp were prospectors searching for gold and one or two selectors looking for cattle runs. In the late 1850s, after gold was discovered at Andersons Creek, near Warrandyte, a wave of fossickers spread east through the hills. Hundreds of these were Chinese.

There was never a great deal of gold in the Gembrook area. A few lucky souls made a living from the alluvial deposits in the creeks but, by 1870, the prospectors had moved on, chasing their dreams. A few had gone back to Melbourne to take up jobs still vacant after the gold rushes had brought the city almost to a standstill. Some of these remembered and talked about the deep red soils around Gembrook. After the passing of the Land Act of 1869 there was another great movement into the hills, this time in search of land. Thousands of men had given up the hunt for gold and had turned their hands to the axe and the plough.

In the early years of the 1870s the land around Gembrook was opened up. In April 1874 the Reverend J. E. Bromby pegged out the area where the township now stands. Alexander Crichton opened a school. Bromby built a church. Gembrook was becoming civilised. The church is, incidentally, well-preserved and still in use.

At about this time there was also some alluvial tin-mining in the creeks and the gem-stones which gave Gembrook its name were attracting fossickers still.

Sawmilling soon became a major industry. Before the land was cleared the forest contained valuable stands of messmate, white gum, stringy-bark, mountain ash, peppermint and blackwood. In the deeper gullies some of these trees rose over ninety metres towards the sun. This was at a time of rapid building in Melbourne and there was a great demand for good, straight timber.

Around Dandenong there was a large trade in redgum logs for wharves and for street paving, but the wood for homes and shops came down from the hills. There was also a strong local demand. Slabs eighteen to twenty centimetres wide were cut and used in much the same way as weatherboards are now. Flooring often consisted of slabs thirty centimetres wide and many roofs were 'tiled' with wooden shingles. Timber was also used for fencing the new farmlands. Wire was unobtainable.

Pit-sawing was the most popular method of reducing the big logs to useful timber. This involved rolling the log over a long, deep pit and sawing it lengthwise with a ripsaw two metres long. One man worked above the log and another below it, in the pit and half-smothered with sawdust.

There were several main mills in the area and most had their own horse-drawn tramways. Timber was railed to Melbourne when the 'iron horse' replaced the much slower bullock-teams. In the 1890s timber prices fell as the demand dropped away again and Melbourne headed into a depression. Scantling fetched as little as 5s 6d per 100 super feet at the railhead, and, as prices dropped, so did wages. A head 'feller' earned £1 4s for a six-day week; a bullock-driver was paid around £1 weekly. Worst off was the 'dusty', the rouseabout who stoked the boilers and docked wood. He was paid the princely sum of 2s 6d per week, with a 4 lb loaf of bread thrown in. At this time such a loaf was worth 4 1/2d.

One mill, about eleven kilometres north of Nar Nar Goon, was a model of efficiency. Built in 1896, with its own tramway system, it maintained an output of 5,000 super feet per day. This was a very great output in those days and its equivalent is not inconsiderable today.

The opening of the narrow-gauge railway from Ferntree Gully to Gembrook in 1900 coincided with the extension of Melbourne's sewerage system. The demand for timber for the sewerage works and the cheap transport offered by the railway, meant a revival of the timber industry. The railway itself provided employment for fifty or sixty men for five or six years. The railway also meant cheaper goods for housewives. Before the line was opened, most supplies were brought up from Pakenham by pack-horse or bullock dray. This added to the cost.

Cheese cost 7d per lb, butter 1s per lb and tea is 6d per lb. Jam was 10d for a 2 lb jar (the jar would now be worth a great deal as a collector's item, for few survived). Bread was up to $3\frac{1}{2}$ d for a loaf. Beef cost about 10d for 5 lb. Those were the days!

Sugar cost only is 9d for 6 lb; clay pipes were 1d each; candles were 1s 6d the half-dozen, cigarettes were 8d per pack and you could still smoke them without being made to feel guilty; 3 lb of chops would cost a single shilling and salmon was only 2d a tin. Clothes, too, seemed cheap by our standards. A shirt at 3s 6d seems a bargain, as does a suit for £3. Remember, though, that £3 was three weeks' wages for a bullock driver. A 'truckie' today would go a deathly shade of pale at the idea of paying three weeks' wages for a suit!

The bullockies were important people in those hills, too. Initially they carried in almost all supplies. They helped clear the land and they carted timber to the mills. They carried timber to Melbourne and helped build the railway line that replaced them. Towing huge iron scoops they carved out the cuttings for the permanent way and the roads. Even grapes and wine were carried by bullock drays in the days when De Baveys winery and vineyard were still in operation.

Bullocky Bill Robinson, last of the local bullockies, died in 1971. Before his death he led the grand parade at the Royal Melbourne Show, driving a team belonging to the late Councillor Wally Legg.

Gembrook is now a peaceful and settled community. It has not yet felt the thrust of the urban problems experienced in the hills to the west. Timber is still being worked, but the hills are patterned with the red squares of cultivation. There is a strong spirit of community, perhaps grown out of the interdependence of the early pioneering families. A hundred years of effort have borne fruit in the beautiful hills and valleys of Gembrook.

35 Two Great Fire Disasters in West Gippsland

The summer of 1898, the year of the great fires, was a time of disaster for Gippsland. Trains caught fire and arrived in stations with carriages alight. Wooden culverts were afire. Passengers were hurt. Finally, the main Gippsland Railway was closed. The whole of central Gippsland was ablaze, along with much of the remainder of the State. Ships in Bass Strait had problems navigating as dense smoke hid the sun and the coastline.

Warragul township suffered little damage, though for a time it was impossible to enter or leave the town, ringed as it was by flames. Poowong was burnt out. Many lesser settlements died in the holocaust. People looking at the cleared land of today cannot readily imagine the dense forests which covered the area before the turn of the century.

Before 1851, Charles Joseph Latrobe had warned that the 'Colony has a great potential for fires … much of it is remote from any settlement and … covered by various types of forest'. In the year of 1851 the infant Port Phillip District was ravaged by great bushfires.

These were probably worse than the 1939 fires but no-one will ever know their extent or the death toll. There were already many people scattered throughout the bush; settlers had taken up runs all across the State. Prospectors were working the creeks deep in the mountains; the Aboriginal population was still numerous; surveyors and explorers still entered the bush. Certainly a number must have been trapped and burnt but that number will always remain a mystery.

The first fire brigades were formed by insurance companies. The first 'formal' brigades in country areas were at Geelong, Bendigo and Creswick in 1854 and in Ballarat in 1856. Many towns then formed their own brigades as soon as water supplies were available. Usually, municipal councils formed and started the brigades by providing a hose, hose reel, fire hooks and other basic equipment. From then on the brigades relied on their own ingenuity and occasional grants from councils and insurance companies.

The fire brigade competitions so popular now are a very real part of maintaining efficiency. The first competition I know of was held in 1873 and involved all the brigades in Melbourne. Exactly one hundred years later another great competition filled the streets of Dandenong with volunteer firemen.

In 1890 Parliament established the Country Fire Brigades Board to control brigades in the cities and towns outside Melbourne. The cost of the first year of operation was £13,295. Of this, the State Government contributed £2,006 4s 9d. Today the cost is about $5

million, and, if all the volunteers were paid for their time, the cost
would rise to much more than $150 million!

The initial cost and the subsequent expenses were all more than
recouped when fires again swept the state in 1898. In 1933 the
number of rural brigades had become so great that the Bush Fire
Brigades Committee was formed. It was this committee which tried
to organise the defence against the 1939 fires.

In January of 1939, several fires, nearly all man-started, spread
until they joined. There was no stopping them. Soon, almost the
whole State was ablaze. Ships in Bass Strait idled along using their
lights and foghorns in the smoke. Even in New Zealand the sky
was darkened by the smoke in the atmosphere. Seventy-one people
died. All the men of the brigades could do was protect small pockets
where there was some chance of success.

Much of the remainder was left to burn. Noojee was a classic
example of courage and grim determination in the face of an
unbeatable foe. Almost the whole town was destroyed and as the
defended perimeter shrank the firefighters withdrew slowly, fighting
all the way. Most knew that if the fire swept over them there would
be no escape. Tradition has it that only the hotel was saved.

There was a Royal Commission set up to inquire into the fires. As
a result of its findings the Country Fire Authority was set up in 1944.
In that year there were 185 town brigades and 727 rural brigades. In
1974 there were 1049 altogether. Today the Country Fire Authority
controls more than 1700 vehicles and 3,000 radio sets, and there are
nearly 120,000 men involved in its operations. This huge organisation
has become one of the world's most efficient fire-fighting services.

This efficiency was proven in 1968-69. Otherwise, the fires in
that season should have been worse than even the 1898 and 1939
disasters. On one infamous day, 8 January 1969, there were 253 fires
burning in Victoria and twenty-one of these were declared 'major
fires'. Despite great heat and strong winds, all were brought under
control. Twenty-one people died, but it is certain that without the
prompt and efficient responses of the Country Fire Authority the
loss of life would have been much greater. Every year, it probably
saves more than its own cost in property alone.

There have been many tales of heroism arising from the great
fires, of course, and many other brave deeds have gone unrecorded.

One that we do know about is that of Captain John Fowler of the Warragul Fire Brigade. Captain Fowler twice galloped through the dense, burning bush around Warragul to effect a double rescue. For 100 kilometres south of Warragul the forests were ablaze. They were so dense that effective firefighting was impossible.

These forests were studded with the lonely huts of isolated settlers. Five kilometres south of the township was the home of a settler named Loader. He was crippled and had stayed at home to mind the youngest child while Mrs Loader took the others on her shopping trip into Warragul. In the township, the now-distraught woman realised that her home was surrounded by an apparently impenetrable wall of flame. She pleaded with Captain Fowler to go to the rescue.

At nine o'clock that night, as soon as the defence of the township was secure, and against the advice of other firefighters, Fowler rode off into the burning bush in search of Loader and any other survivors. He found Loader crouched in the ruins of his home, huddled over the child. 'Good God', Loader cried, according to one account. 'How did you get here? You'll never get out! What is your mission?'

Fowler answered by taking the child and wrapping it in his leather coat. He galloped to safety through the flames with only a singlet to protect his chest and back from the heat. Handing over the child he wheeled his horse and returned to rescue the father. The child and Captain Fowler both recovered, but, sadly, the crippled settler lingered a few weeks and then succumbed to the effects of his terrible ordeal.

Fowler went on to become a respected businessman in the district and stated that his action was only that of a man doing his duty. His brave deed is only one small part of the chapter of service this state's firefighters have written in the past 120 years.

36 West Gippsland's Grand Old Man of Agriculture

Alexander Patterson was the grand old man of agriculture in West Gippsland. His run was not the largest in the district and other settlers had more money. Yet his influence was felt far beyond the fences of 'St Germaine', his station near Clyde.

He is said to have been the originator of the idea of the Mornington Pastoral and Agricultural Society, from which sprang the Berwick and District Agricultural and Horticultural Society. This latter Society is thus, in a sense, the oldest of its type in Victoria.

A meeting held at Mrs Bowman's inn on the Cardinia Creek, now the Central Hotel at Beaconsfield, resulted in great support for the idea of an agricultural society, the society formally being established at a meeting in Dandenong on 6 October 1856. Patterson was the first secretary and treasurer. Later he became the president and he served on the committee in various roles until 1882. He was regarded as the driving force behind the society and was probably the main reason for its continued success.

Alexander Patterson was born at Blawerie, Berwickshire, Scotland, on 24 January 1813. His grandfather, also named Alexander, was a farmer at Coldingham, Berwickshire, and it was probably from him that young Alex gained his knowledge and love of the land. He left Scotland in 1838 and landed in Adelaide early in 1839. At first he managed a run for a Dr Kelly, but three years later he came to Victoria. In 1948 he was an overseer at 'Glenaroua' station, near what is now Kilmore.

While at 'Glenaroua' he was sent to select 100 rams from John Macarthur's Camden merinos. He drove these back to 'Glenaroua', without the benefit of roads or bridges and with the assistance of only two other men.

His next position was at 'Kout Narien' station, near Kaniva, and then he became manager of 'Kenilworth' station, which occupied some 25500 hectares along the Wannon River. By now he had amassed a considerable knowledge of local conditions and had some small capital behind him. He began to look for a station of his own. In January 1848 he acquired the twenty-three square kilometres of 'St Germaine' station, having been attracted by the abundance of green pasture. This station was on the western edge of what was then known as the Great Swamp.

John Knox's Church in Melbourne was the scene of Patterson's wedding on 20 August 1852. He married Marion McMurtrie, daughter of David and Helen McMurtrie of Dalmellington, Ayrshire, Scotland. Again, one cannot help wondering why there were so many Scots among the pioneers of West Gippsland. They seem to have far outnumbered even the English and the Irish.

On 16 May 1853, their first child was born. Young Thomas was to follow in his father's footsteps as secretary of the Agricultural Society and eventually as a councillor of the Cranbourne Shire. Thomas was also on the original committee of the Cranbourne race course and in 1880 was elected secretary of the National Agricultural Society, which is now the Royal Agricultural Society. In those days the society had a site on St Kilda Road, near Victoria Barracks. Thomas served on the executive of the society until 1910, during which time the present Showgrounds site was bought and the hill which stood where the main arena now is was levelled.

Thomas was married in Cranbourne, by the celebrated Alexander Duff. His bride was Mary Elizabeth Thomson and they were wed on 15 April 1881. Their eldest child, Sydney Wentworth Patterson, later became the first director of the Walter and Eliza Institute of Research in Pathology and Medicine.

The second child of Alexander and Marion was Alexander David Patterson, born at the homestead on 20 November 1858. He became a manager of various branches of the Commercial Bank of Australia and in 1895 was sent to Kalgoorlie. He was associated with various mining ventures in Western Australia for eight years before coming back to Melbourne as a legal manager for various interests. He never seems to have shown any great interest in the agricultural pursuits of his brother and father.

The third child was John Denham Patterson, born at 'St Germaine' on 31 May 1860. He joined the agricultural societies and eventually became a life member of the Royal Agricultural Society. He took up residence at Jesmond Dene, that part of the original 'St Germaine' which lies on the east bank of the Cardinia Creek.

Alexander's fourth child was his only daughter, Helen Richardson Patterson. She was born at the homestead and married Thomas Gray Webster. The wedding was on 19 January 1886. Webster decided to take his young bride to England, but he died in Adelaide on 30 November of that same year. His widow returned to Berwick and eventually became prominent in public affairs. She was secretary of the Red Cross for some years and was on the foundation committee of St Margaret's Ladies College in Berwick.

Meanwhile the original Alexander Patterson had become a figure of considerable public importance. He was on the first council of the

Board of Agriculture, was on the committee of the Port Phillip Society, was a founder of the National (now Royal) Agricultural Society and was a widely-acclaimed judge of livestock at many shows.

He was a member of the first Cranbourne Roads Board in 1861 and was the chairman in 1863. In 1868 he became a councillor when the Roads Board became a Shire Council; he was Shire President in 1872-73. He was also a territorial magistrate and a founder and trustee of the Cranbourne Presbyterian Church.

He died at home on his beloved 'St Germaine' on 29 December 1896, at the ripe old age of eighty-six. His grave is in the Cranbourne cemetery, a fitting resting-place for the man who did so much to promote the rural skills on which the prosperity of the shire has so far been based.

37 Up Came the Squatters

None of the spectacular development of the Great Swamp could have taken place without the courage and perseverance of the first explorers and squatters. Angus McMillan never reached the Great Swamp. Paul Strzelecki passed through it in great haste, battling to reach Western Port before his party became too weak.

The first real exploration began in June 1841. Dr Edward Barker, Albert Brodribb and Edward Hobson, with two Aboriginal guides, walked from Melbourne to Port Albert and back. The names of the two Aborigines are not known, unfortunately. The party suffered great hardship and was close to starvation when the men walked into Port Albert.

The food they carried on their backs had soon been exhausted. As was often the case, the Aborigines saved the lives of the white men by providing food 'off the land' but the whites were unable to eat much of it. We know little about their return journey but we do know that they reached Melbourne safely and that they reported good grazing prospects in Gippsland. The present Princes Highway follows their tracks for some distance.

Soon the first settlers spread out from Dandenong and up from the coast. They tried to avoid the Great Swamp, that vast area of running water, deep mud and impenetrable ti-tree where the mythical bunyip was said to live. Squatters selected land along the coast and in the foothills of the Great Divide to the north. Grantville and Port Albert were two centres for radiating development. Some came down from Drouin and Warragul, or up from Lang Lang, into the Strzelecki Ranges.

Soon the map showed that almost the whole of Gippsland had been taken up, except the dreaded Great Swamp, called by some the Koo Wee Rup Swamp. On the west the swamp was bounded by the 'Gin Gin Bean' and 'St Germaine' stations. On the north were the Toomah, Mt Ararat, Mt Ararat Creek and the legendary 'TYU', the 'Speewah' of Gippsland. On the southern and eastern sides there were Yallock and Torbinnurruck (Tobin Yallock), Toorodan and Mantons. Only the 'TYU' really claimed any part of the swamp.

Dr W. K. Jamieson settled on the Toomuc Creek in October 1839, and there he founded the 'TYU'. The origin of the name is a mystery. William Kerr Jamieson was a man of explosive temper but kind heart. Neil Gunson wrote of him: 'Old Pills [the nickname the good doctor went by] was a choleric, eccentric medical practitioner, who had laid aside his potions and blisters and gathered some flocks of fine sheep, [and] possessed himself of a capital run ... Though blunt ... in his rough exterior dwelt the true milk of human kindness; ever ready to help alleviate the distress and troubles of his fellows, yet never without a grumble that "he would never go again so it was no use sending for him". But go again he did, and no one can tell the good the doctor did in those outlying districts far away from medical help.'

Other squatters in the area were Terence O'Connor, who took up Cardinia Creek No. 1 in September 1838; Robert Henry, whose run was also called Cardinia Creek and who came in October 1842; Alexander Patterson, who took up 'St Germaine' in January 1848 and James Lecky, who took up Panty Gurn Gurn in 1850.

The lives of these men were relatively civilised. Certainly living conditions were rugged by today's standards but there were many home comforts. Most of the squatters came from 'good family backgrounds' and brought with them such things as a knowledge of books and music and the ability to converse well. These were valuable social tools even in those days.

Apparently Richard Corbett was rather an exception. He took over the Rutherford's run near where Tooradin is now, and renamed it Kilmore. His family found it difficult to believe, when they received his letters, that he was even remotely respectable, let alone a gentleman. He wrote to his sister in 1849, two years after he took over the run, that he wanted her to 'hemegrate'. He added: 'I have got one hundred and twenty horned cattle and seven head of hors flesh I keep 5 Servant men and to woman I have one hors team and one teams of Bullocks'.

Things went well for Corbett as he strove to become a gentleman. In 1853 he wrote that he had 'uperds of five Hundred of horned Cattle and 14 horses I milk from 30 to 40 Cows the yer round'. He also wrote that 'I can Ashure you that we grows Everything that Man Can Eat or Beast we grow weet Barley mais oats potatoes Cabbages carots and every thing nesery for lif mor so then what you in ingland I have got A butful vineard which we grood from 4 to 5 hundreds waight thes last 3 years you ned not think any thing of this Cuntry for it is the finest Cuntry in the wool world'.

One does not need to be able to spell to be a capable and courageous settler.

Despite the efforts of the squatters to make their lives more comfortable there were problems, and one of these was the presence of the Aborigines. The Bunuron tribe were generally peaceful but an attempt was made to bring in some Aborigines from Tasmania as a 'civilising influence'. In the first days of October 1840, the Yallock station was attacked by a force of about one hundred Aborigines.

Jamieson, a partner in the station, fired a warning shot above the heads of the marauders. To his credit, he refused to fire directly into the attacking tribesmen, using his rifle like a club on those who tried to enter his hut. All the other huts were gutted and wrecked. The raiders were more interested in robbery than in murder. They stripped the station bare and then made off into the bush. It was then discovered that they had been camped on a nearby creek for two days without any of the whites suspecting their presence.

Protector Thomas, whose job it was to care for the Aborigines, rode down to see that no revenge was taken. Apparently the raiding party was really seeking a body of the Port Phillip blacks to take revenge of their own for a murder committed earlier.

Few of the stolen items were recovered but, during the raid, one astute Irishman at least saved his watch. He fled toward the creek, pursued by two Aborigines. His clothes hindered his passage and as he neared the water he stripped them off. The first of the two blacks promptly seized his trousers, with his watch in the pocket. This was too much. The Irishman turned back, knocked the two blacks down, recovered his watch and plunged into the water, making good his escape. History does not record whether the watch survived the wetting it received.

38 Stop-Start Railway

Between the Depression and the Second World War, roads in Gippsland were greatly improved and trucks of greater efficiency and capacity were entering the road trade. This was the pattern all over the State. Many small branch railways had to be closed because they could no longer compete. The branch line to Strzelecki began closing down in 1930, though the closure of the last working section did not occur until 4 February 1959.

Back in 1914 there was a need to send a branch line into the rich dairying country that lay between the main Gippsland line and the Great Southern Railway. A start was made on construction in 1915 but a shortage of labour caused by the war forced a halt in April 1916. Work started again in 1919 and, after another pause in 1920, the line was opened to 'Strezlecki' on 29 June 1922. (It was not until 1929 that the Victorian Railways changed the name of the terminus to 'Strzelecki', the correct spelling.) This stop-start approach meant that it took seven years to bring the line from Koo Wee Rup to Strzelecki, on the top of the Ranges, the line being built by the Railway Construction Branch and costing £586,990.

There were several problems to be overcome in raising the line from the valley of the Lang Lang River at Triholm to the high township of Strzelecki but these were overcome. The Koo Wee Rup Swamp had been drained by this time so it presented no real difficulty. A low embankment was all that was needed. There were bridges over the No. 4 Drain and the No. 6 Drain, the 'Four' and the 'Six' to the locals.

Top: The store and smithy built by Ures at 'Silver Wells' (see Story 33).
Bottom: The butcher's shop at the end of the original store (see Story 33)

*Top: Construction works on the new bridge at San Remo, 1967 (see Story 39).
Bottom: The old San Remo bridge being dismantled. The new bridge can be seen in the
background (see Story 39). Photos: Country Roads Board, Victoria*

These were small bridges but the crossing of the Lang Lang River at Heath Hill called for a much bigger bridge. Nearby, the Western Port road was carried over the line on another bridge.

The line was of fairly light construction, the ballast being local gravel. The availability of this was one of the main reasons for the construction of the line, as gravel was shipped out to other places. Passenger traffic was a minor consideration. The other significant reason was, of course, the need to provide fairly fast transport to Melbourne for dairy produce.

The gravel and sand were so important that two sidings were built near Bayles to cater for the trade. From 1926 to 1932 the Plowright Sand Company and the Koo Wee Rup Water-washed Sand Company used these sidings to load sand excavated from the original bed of the Bunyip River. This river has long since disappeared, the water it carried now being borne to the sea by the Main Drain. The gravel pits doffed about the swamp are clues to the original course. This sand and gravel bore topaz and even occasional sapphires and zircons. Who knows how many gemstones may have been carted up to the railway and spread among the ballast?

Each mining company built tram tracks to bring the sand to the sidings. The locations of these sidings are now know to only a few, and even the locals argue about where they were. Stations eventually built along the line were Koo Wee Rup, Bayles, Catani, Yannathan, Heath Hill, Triholm and Strzelecki. The embankments built near the Triholm station are still very clearly visible near the Lang Lang River on the Drouin-to-Korumburra road.

At first there was very little passenger traffic; a goods train which ran three times a week merely had a passenger carriage attached. This 'mixed goods' entered service in 1922, connecting with mainline trains at Koo Wee Rup. In 1924 a 'milk train' ran every morning except Sundays, as far as Yannathan; this service was available until 1930 when it was discontinued because of a lack of demand.

On 22 November 1930, competition from road traffic led to the closing of the steep Triholm-Strzelecki section. 7 August 1941, saw the closing of the Yannathan-Triholm section. This time the reason was the erosion of the river banks near the Heath Hill bridge. It was decided that the limited traffic would not justify the cost of repairs. At the time of closing there were only two trains weekly to Triholm;

when the section closed the service on the line was reduced to one train to Yannathan each Wednesday.

The Bayles-Yannathan section was closed on 15 April 1950, again because of the lack of traffic and despite the strong protests of many residents. The remaining section, between Bayles and Koo Wee Rup, managed to stay open until 4 February 1959. The longer life of this section was brought about by the potato and sand traffic and the agitation of local residents.

In all, the full forty-nine kilometres of this 'mini-railway' were open for only eight years, but the final section stayed open for thirty-seven years. In that time it did much to aid the growth and stability of the small communities it served.

39 How They Tamed the Eastern Crossing

The Eastern Passage between Phillip Island and the mainland is a spectacular stretch of water and it has played a colourful part in Gippsland's history. HMS *Lady Nelson* anchored there in 1801 while exploring the coast and Western Port under the command of Lieutenant James Grant, R.N. It appears that George Bass also entered the passage and we know that it was used by sealers and whalers. There was a sealers' hut at Newhaven in very early days.

From the time that men settled on Phillip Island the Eastern Passage has had to be crossed with supplies. Normally small boats were used but there have been a few remarkable exceptions. One man who stole some chickens from a Chinese family at Newhaven was pursued by the knife-wielding Orientals and was cornered on the jetty. Acknowledging that discretion was the better part of valour he abandoned his loot and plunged into the water. He made the crossing safely.

Another story from a later date tells of a young man working on the building of the famous suspension bridge who attended a dance on the mainland with his workmates. He escorted a young lady home and his friends could not find him when their boat was due to leave. In the wee small hours he made his way back to the island — along the single strand of cable that had been rigged across the passage.

Harry Rosevear of Bass used to swim his draught horses over to Woody Point (Newhaven) for contract ploughing. As well an elaborate technique was devised for bringing cattle across. A yard was built on the beach with a long, narrow race leading down to the low-water mark. At low tide, if the weather was calm enough (and it often was not), men would take a rowing boat to the end of the race. The race would be opened and cattle, usually very wild indeed, would charge down the slope to attack the men in the boat. Before they reached them, of course, the cattle would be swimming and could fairly easily be herded to the other side.

There were many stories of close escapes during this process. Men fell from the boat in the path of the cattle. Changes in the current could sweep the tiring beasts off course. Sudden winds could make the crossing treacherous.

Eventually a series of punts came into use. These were flat-ended barges which were towed by a motor launch. The launch would tow the punt towards the landing-ramp at high speed and then swing to one side, casting off the tow cable. It was hoped that the momentum would then carry the barge up to the landing. Sometimes this was unsuccessful and the currents would land the drifting barge anywhere on the beach. This meant that the cargo, often including motor vehicles, would have to be carefully ferried across the often-soft sand. On one occasion a rather tipsy traveller managed to drive his car off the punt into five metres of water. Eventually, both he and the car were recovered, relatively undamaged.

In 1930 there was an experimental attempt to move the barges by hand-operated winch but this was unsuccessful. By this time Phillip Island was a popular spot and it was apparent that a better system was needed. Richard A. Grayden, an early settler, was convinced that a bridge could be built and he worked for many years to gather support for the idea. The Bridge League was formed on 27 April 1937, with 388 members, Grayden among them. On 11 November 1938, at a public meeting attended by Albert Dunstan, the Premier of Victoria, the people of Phillip Island gave the idea almost unanimous support.

The first pile was driven not long after and the bridge was opened on Friday 29 November 1940. It was a spectacular feat of engineering — 538 metres long and carrying a roadway over five metres. The towers carrying the suspension cables rose almost thirty-four metres from the sea; the eighteen arches on the island side of the main span each covered eighteen metres and there were three spans of fifteen metres each on the mainland end.

The main span was supported on twelve cables bought secondhand in Sydney after the Sydneysiders completed their famous 'coathanger', with the centre span of the bridge having a minimum clearance of twelve metres above the water. The whole bridge was built for £62,000, perhaps the most spectacular statistic of all.

The Country Roads Board designed the new bridge when the old suspension bridge began to show its age. The new bridge is concrete, with a main arch of over twenty metres and a clearance of twelve metres. It is a beautiful bridge but it somehow lacks the charm of its predecessor. If you ever find yourself under the bridge in a boat you will appreciate the cathedral-like beauty of the concrete arches, but a strong current makes it hard to appreciate this for long. It also led to problems in the design of the bridge.

Now, where Grant and Bass ventured, where the sealers and whalers plied their trade, where the Cleelands and the McHaffies struggled with their wild cattle, where the punts were hauled across against the current, the motorist races across a highway suspended in the sky, perhaps with a passing comment on the scenery or the tide.

It seems a shame, somehow.

40 The French Explorer Who Sailed the Gippsland Coast

We have all heard of the famous Matthew Flinders and his friend George Bass — their exploits have become a legend. We know about Lieutenants Grant and Murray and their explorations of Bass Strait, Western Port and Port Phillip Bay. The names they put on the map have endured.

One explorer has been forgotten. The names he wrote across his charts are no longer used or even remembered. Even in his own country of France he is virtually unknown. For various reasons this intrepid explorer, Thomas Nicolas Baudin, has never been given full credit for his magnificent journey to what the English called New Holland and the French called 'Terre Napoleon'.

Fittingly enough for a man destined to become one of the great navigators, Baudin was born on an island at St-Martin de Re on 17 February 1756. His father, Francois, was a merchant and, apart from the fact that he sold supplies to a lighthouse, the family had no connection with the sea.

When he was twenty-one years old Baudin was on his way to the East Indies as a soldier. At the beginning of the American Revolution he had become a naval officer but he was stripped of his command by a conspiracy of officers of more noble birth. His colourful career then continued in the service of Joseph II, Emperor of Austria, commanding an Austrian ship. He was sent to the Indian Ocean in 1786 and the Pacific Ocean in 1789, collecting botanic specimens.

On 20 April 1792, Baudin left Italy in the ship *Jardiniere*. In the Strait of Gibraltar a French vessel surrendered to him, his first indication that France was at war. He hastened to Malaga to offer his services to his mother country but a bureaucrat told him that regulations prevented his enlistment. Disgusted, he continued his voyage and on 2 April 1793, he reached the Cape of Good Hope.

The voyage was a disaster. He was arrested by the British at Bombay, forced to turn back from New Holland by two hurricanes, shipwrecked, and finally taken to the United States of America. He returned to France in 1795. After another voyage to the West Indies for botanic specimens he spent much time and effort persuading the French authorities to allow him to sail to New Holland, and that is where the relevance of his story to the history of Victoria begins.

Baudin left Le Havre on 19 October 1800, in command of the *Geographe*. He first sighted the coast of New Holland on 27 May 1801. It is only the part of his voyage which lay along the coast of Gippsland we are interested in so I shall not include any details of his voyage around Van Diemens Land and north to Port Jackson. However, he did have many adventures during this period. These include stories of the discovery of a girl stowaway, disease, drownings and near-shipwreck.

By 29 November 1802, Baudin was again tacking among the rocky islands of Bass Strait, troubled by strong currents and foul weather. His subordinate, Captain Hamelin, who commanded the *Naturaliste* which was sailing in convoy, signalled that one of the crew had struck an officer. Baudin ordered the sailor fifty strokes of the lash and warned that this would not affect the judgement to which he would have to submit on return to France. At times, Baudin was inclined to wish that Hamelin had not accompanied him.

On one occasion, while changing course, the *Naturaliste* nearly collided with Baudin's ship, the *Geographe*. Hamelin hauled his helm hard over and swung his ship in a tight circle. At first he avoided the *Geographe* but he did not correct his helm in time and on the second turn he did collide. Baudin was not amused.

Baudin spent several days among the islands off Wilsons Promontory, many of which were not shown on Flinders' charts. He named most of them but very few of the names he gave were ever officially recognised. On 28 March 1802, he approached Wilsons Promontory from the south and sailed up the west side of it. He sailed into Waratah Bay and described West Point, now Cape Liptrap. He lay offshore during the night and next day sailed west to Venus Bay and Cape Patterson, reporting that Venus Bay seemed larger than the English chart showed.

He noted: 'The land ... is a good height ... [and] a fairly considerable way inland one can see a long range of mountains. They are of medium height. In the afternoon we ... passed very close to a large, jutting point of land, which was maintained to be the island that forms Westernport.' There was some dispute among the crew as to whether this was really what we now call Cape Woolamai. Next day, 30 March, the issue was resolved.

At eleven o'clock Baudin saw an opening which he identified as Western Port but he made no effort to enter it. He stood a fair distance offshore but insisted that the charts made by Flinders, Grant and Murray were wrong in several respects. He then sailed west past the entrance to Port Phillip Bay, which he apparently did not see though it was shown on the charts he had. He named Cap des Representations and Point de la Plate-forme, possibly those we now know as Cape Schank and Point Nepean, though this is guesswork.

He wrote: 'The coast was agreeable-looking and had no obvious hazards ... [and] we noted some smoke which indicated that this part of the continent was inhabited'. What he called Le Coin de Mire became Curtis Island. Les Deux Freres became Cone Island and Sugarloaf, though Flinders had called them Two Peaks. What Baudin called Cone Island is now named Rodondo Island.

Baudin next sailed to King Island, which he explored, and on 19 December he was again off Wilsons Promontory. He knew that he was close to Western Port but the wind changed and he returned to King Island. At this stage he seems not to have been in any great hurry. Even in those early days he met white men in the Strait, and sealers (he called them 'fishermen') sold him kangaroo, emu and wombat meat to supplement his provisions.

Soon after, he sailed west to Kangaroo Island, South Australia, and passed out of Bass Strait for the last time. *Le Geographe* reached Ile de France on 7 August 1803. Six weeks later, on 16 September, Baudin died of a fever he had caught in Timor on the long voyage home.

41 Nyerri-Warren

Probably no-one 'will ever know how Narre Warren came by its name. There are as many theories as there are local historians and they 'have heads on 'em like mice'. There are four main contentions however. Each has an army of supporters, and the debate has become a little warmer now that Narre Warren is the heart of the sprawling new city of Berwick.

'Nyerriwarren' is a native word for 'red hills'. It is possible that the name was used for the area generally. The soil is red in a number of places around Narre Warren and Berwick and they are on the first foothills to the north-west of the flat land that stretches down to the Koo Wee Rup Swamp. This is the least supportable theory.

Some say that the name comes from two Aboriginal words meaning 'bad water' and it is true that the area south of the railway line was once a large swamp of brackish water. But the theory which seems to have the most support nowadays is that the name was somehow derived from 'Narre Nareen'. This Aboriginal name is believed to have meant 'small hills' and to have referred to the foothills of the Dandenong Ranges. There is no real explanation offered for the alteration of the name.

The fourth theory, and the one to which I subscribe, is that the name was chosen by Captain Lonsdale, as far back as 1837, when it was decided that a depot for the Native Police should be established in the Corhan-Warrabul area. This depot provided the origin of the 'Police Paddocks' near Dandenong. Lonsdale is believed to have taken the native word for 'she-oke' and the word for ocean', 'Narre' and 'Warren', to make an alliterative name which may have sounded pleasant but which had little local relevance.

There were she-okes in the area. When in flower, they were once described as looking like a river of blood flowing to the sea from a sacred hill north of Narre Warren where there were a number of tribal fights. The origin of the name does not really matter, though. It provides little more than an interesting background to a colourful history.

Lonsdale's proposal for a Native Police Depot was agreed to in 1841 and the Government of New South Wales voted £1,000 for its establishment. Captain Henry Pultney Dana was to be Officer in Charge. He was assisted by William Thomas, the Protector of Aborigines at that time, William Dana, his brother, and a Senior Constable named Walsh. A native tribal chief called Billibellary was appointed to arrange the recruiting of suitable natives. He selected twelve but by 1847 there were only four still serving. They were being paid threepence per day.

Two colourful incidents marked the history of the Depot. Senior Constable Walsh shot William Dana while on parade one morning. It is believed that the moody Walsh was jealous of Dana. The victim eventually recovered but Walsh, despite his plea of insanity, was found guilty of doing grievous bodily harm and was sentenced to ten years with hard labour.

The second incident occurred with the report of a white woman who was believed to be a captive of the Aborigines somewhere near the Gippsland Lakes. Possibly she was a survivor from the wreck of the *Britannia* or the *Britomart*. She was thought to be held by an Aborigine called Bunjalecua, but although he was captured the woman was not found. The story has it that the woman was taken by Bunjalecua's brother who murdered her when another native tried to steal her from him. Some reports say that her body and that of a child were discovered at Jemmys Point on the lakes; others say that only a dress and child's shoe were found. This has never been resolved.

'Brechin', the home of John Lloyd, was originally the home of Thomas Walton. Walton was possibly the first settler of Narre Warren and called his home 'Holly Green'. When he sold it in 1880 the buyer was Sydney John Webb.

Webb gave his name to the main street, the street he built, in Narre Warren. The land between 'Brechin' and the railway station was part of 'Roseneath', owned by Captain Wauchope. Webb arranged for the construction of a road through 'Roseneath' and arranged a public subscription to pay for the railway station. He also donated land for the school and the public hall. That part of the Narre Warren Recreation Reserve which holds the Memorial Gates was also donated by Webb, and in 1890 he planted an avenue of oak trees along the highway which became a beautiful landmark. (Unfortunately the Country Roads Board removed half the avenue.)

Most of the streets in Narre Warren came into existence when Wilmore and Randall opened their Civic Centre Estates. They used the names of prominent early settlers — Woodley, Kent, Moran, Hillbrick, Sweeney, Lloyd, Richardson, Wauchope, Nobelius and Keys.

There was a troop of Light Horse (Narre Warren Troop, 5th Squadron, 10th Australian Light Horse) raised in the 1900s of which the members were such skilled horsemen that they were often called upon to provide guards-of-honour for visiting dignitaries. These included Lord Tennyson during his term as Governor-General; Sir Henry Rawson, the Governor of New South Wales; Sir Thomas Gibson Carmichael while he was Governor of Victoria and even the famous Admiral Sperry of the United States Navy

There was some confusion over the use of the name 'Narre Warren' which was reflected in the names of the schools. The name had first been applied to the settlement that is now Narre Warren North. When the railway was opened in 1878 a new town began to grow up near the station using the same name though it was five kilometres south of its parent village. For a time the problem was solved by using the names 'New Narre Warren' and 'Old Narre Warren', but this was not very satisfactory. The school at Narre Warren North was known as Narre Warren State School until 1925 and the school at Narre Warren was called Narre Warren Railway Station State School. Now, to add to this, or to commemorate it, the new school being built south of the railway is being named Narre

Warren Station Primary School.

No. 2924, the school in Webb Street, was applied for in 1886 by S. J. Webb and others. It was opened on 20 March 1889. Until then, the children of the district travelled to Berwick or to Narre Warren North for their education. The original building was a single schoolroom with a three-roomed residence attached. It served until 1929, when the present school building was erected and the schoolroom was detached from the residence and transferred to No. 3033, Beaconsfield State School, where it is in use to this day.

Narre Warren is now growing very rapidly again but it went into a decline between the two World Wars. It once had a butcher's shop north of the highway (now the Trewin home), a bakery run by Mr Woodley whose son, Albert, was a well-known music-hall comedian, and a general store. There was also a motor garage which was burnt down in 1971 while housing the business of Noel Gould.

The Mechanics Institute was the scene of constant social activity by the end of the First World War. It housed a very large library which was later donated to the Repatriation General Hospital at Heidelberg and a billiard table to play on which one had to book about a week ahead. Now the old Institute is again in almost constant use.

Self-help between individuals and between organisations in Narre Warren has always been evident. The road to the railway was built by public subscription; the kindergarten and infant welfare centre were the result of a long campaign by a few ladies; the recreation ground was bought by the Progress Association and handed over to the Council and the fire brigade raises most of its own funds. When the football area was upgraded it was local labour that made it possible; when a pavilion was called for, local people guaranteed the money. In this sense at least, Narre Warren is still carrying on the tradition laid down by its first settlers.

42 Leongatha Labour Colony

The prosperity of Leongatha rests upon the hard work and the skills of the dairy farmers in the surrounding district. They owe the success they enjoyed in turn to those who cleared and developed the land. One such group was the Leongatha Labour Colony, now almost forgotten but a vital part of Leongatha's past.

The good pasture that surrounds this pretty town was once a dense jungle of eucalypt with matted undergrowth. In 1904 James Smith wrote: 'In whatever direction the visitor to Leongatha may turn, nothing but trees will meet his eye, so dense that the township resembles a clearing in the midst of an unending forest of sombre gum trees … the thickly waving forest of trees conceals from view the … surrounding country'.

In the 1890s Victoria suffered a severe economic depression which left many people out of work. In some areas the effect was almost as bad as in the Great Depression of the 1930s. The Charity Organisation Society decided to do something about it. One member remembered seeing labour colonies in Germany and suggested that the idea might work here. The basis of the colony was the employment in clearing and farming of men who had no jobs. Their employment was co-operative and the scheme was supposed to be self-supporting. In June 1893, the scheme was formally begun under the control of the Minister for Lands and with the full blessing of the Government. The first superintendent was Colonel Goldstein, who was in charge until 1903 when the Labour Colony was placed directly under the control of the Lands Department and worked by the then Director of Agriculture.

The site chosen for the beginning was over two kilometres from the town on the Mirboo Road. It held 332 hectares of chocolate soil, perhaps not quite as good as that of the Marks brothers next door. The first cultivation was on the banks of Coalition Creek, where tents were erected and the draftees were set to work clearing the forest. Soon they were able to begin putting up permanent houses.

A sawmill was built to handle the timber. At the end of twelve months most of the area was cleared. A residence had been built for Mr Ure, a member of a family that helped pioneer the Gembrook area. By 1904 the colony had a well-developed orchard, large poultry runs, a huge kitchen garden, a workshop, stores and an office. The office was occupied by a Mr Campbell who had been hired to act as an accountant. There was also a general store, a blacksmith and a bakery. The men ate in a large mess hall on the same diet scale as the Navy — the cook was a ship's cook who had been found without employment.

Stables were built for the fourteen horses of the colony. An 8 h.p. steam engine was obtained to run a flax treatment plant, the engine being also used to crush linseed and to manufacture oil-cake and hemp fibre. This wide diversification was one of the most important aspects of the colony.

Originally begun solely to provide employment, it slowly became a kind of experimental and training farm. The farm produced about ten cans of cream per week in 1904. The creamery was probably one of the best-equipped in the State, with its own tramway, testing apparatus, and even steam-driven separators.

There was provision for the underground storage of more than 200 tonnes of silage. Peas, beans, oats and maize were grown to be added to the silage and other vegetables were grown for sale in the town and to supply the mess kitchen. There were thirty Berkshire sows for breeding and usually about 150 baconers were kept at any one time. The dairy herd ranged between sixty and 100 and there was a bullock-team to supplement the work of the horses. Tobacco was grown but this proved to be a failure.

Ten or twelve new colonists arrived each week. After applying for their positions they were carefully screened. For the first week they received no pay and in the second week they earnt 6d. This was progressively increased until it reached the maximum of 5s. When a man had £2 to his credit he was expected to leave and make room for someone else; if he was unable to find work 'on the outside' he was eligible to re-apply after one month. Between the beginning of the colony in 1893 and 16 December 1904, 6100 men passed through it. There were 18866 applications.

In many ways the colony became a College of Agriculture for the unemployed because many of the men became so fond of life on the land that they never returned to the city, seeking farm work instead. The wide diversity of skills they picked up in the Labour Colony made them excellent farm workers.

The average cost of the scheme to the Government was about £3,000 per year, a large part of this money being spent in the small township of Leongatha, with obvious benefits for local traders. The significance is easily seen when one realises that the colony spent more than £1,000 a year, plus what the men spent out of their earnings, in a township which had a population in 1904 of only 700.

The Leongatha Labour Colony no longer exists, of course, and Leongatha is a prosperous and substantial town surrounded by hundreds of square kilometres of prime pasture. It is as well, perhaps, to pause sometimes and think about the immense effort that went into preparing that pasture.

43 A Seat in Parliament—for 368 Votes

To many early Gippslanders, political thinking was something which took place in the cities and had little to do with the man on the land. Busy clearing scrub, fencing, building a home, planting pasture and generally becoming established, the majority of settlers had little time for such complexities.

Once established, though, the settler often began to wonder about the possibility of a new road or a railway, or a school, and this oft-times turned his thoughts to politics. By voting, or becoming a candidate, the new settler usually became involved in politics one way or another once he felt that he could spare the time. The area now known as Gippsland has been represented at State and Federal level by a number of particularly capable men, but they have rarely been able to gain for the province the recognition it deserves.

The *Victorian Constitution Act* was passed in 1855, dividing Gippsland into two electorates called Gipps' Land and Alberton. It is easy to imagine the frustration of settlers seeking representation when the electorates were so large and roads were almost nonexistent.

The first representative for Gipps' Land was John King, who took his seat in the Legislative Assembly in October 1856, and held it until 7 November 1857. His successor was John Johnson, who held the seat until 1859. In that year, Gipps' Land was divided into North Gippsland and South Gippsland.

Angus McMillan represented South Gippsland for a year but found that battling droughts, floods and Aborigines was much easier than battling councils, committees and cabinets. He went 'back to the bush' in 1860. He was replaced by a friend, Dr Hedley, the Sale doctor and prospector after whom the township of Hedley was named. Hedley held the seat until 1864, when he was ousted by a grazier, Peter Snodgrass.

In 1869 Snodgrass lost to Dr Macartney and he, in turn, lost to F. C. Mason in 1871. Macartney got back in 1877 though he polled only 368 votes! Mason then lodged a petition against the return of Macartney on the grounds that the latter was a Minister of Religion at the time of the election and was therefore ineligible. Another election was held and again Macartney won.

He lived only until May the following year, 1878, and Mason won the resultant by-election, becoming the representative for quite some time. There were two elections in 1880 and Mason won both, one election being on 28 February and another on 14 July. At a further election he was returned unopposed but he was defeated in March 1886. The victor on this occasion was Arthur Champion Groom, a very well-known auctioneer.

Groom held the seat until 1889 when yet another redistribution took place, and South Gippsland was divided to create the new seats of Gippsland West and Gippsland South. Groom stood for Gippsland West and won it, while F. C. Mason re-entered Parliament by winning Gippsland South. On 26 April 1892, Groom was defeated by George J. Turner, a selector from the Gainsborough Flats, near Darnum. Turner was a Labor man and won again in 1894 and 1897. His opponent in 1897 was again Groom, who after this defeat turned his interest to Federal politics and was successful at his first attempt.

In 1900 Turner retired from politics and his seat was taken by Arthur George Nichols of Drouin West. In this election John Emanuel Mackay stood for the first time and was defeated. In October 1902, he stood again and this time he was successful, representing Gippsland West until he died in 1924. Only in 1911 was he opposed and on that occasion he scored an outright victory over his two opponents.

These are basically the dry bones of the early Gippsland political scene, but there was much more colour than I have suggested. It was the astute use of politics, for instance, that enabled the citizens of Drouin and Warragul to have the railway re-routed through their towns after the original plan showed it as passing well to the south.

Sadly, most of the stories of the personalities and the clashes between them have been lost to us. Voting figures show how thinly the population of West Gippsland was spread, while the original electorate of South Gippsland had only six polling booths until 1877. These were at Alberton, Brandy Creek (Warragul), Palmerston (near Welshpool), Stockyard Creek (Foster), Tarraville and Woodside.

44 March for Life from Sandy Point

At noon on Monday, 24 January 1836, the midsummer silence of Western Port was shattered by the rattle of anchor chains and the shouts of command. The 300-tonne barque *Norval*, under the command of Captain Robert Coltish, was anchoring off Sandy Point.

The ship was carrying a cargo of sheep for the Port Phillip Association and aboard her was Joseph Tice Gellibrand, the *de facto* head of the association now that the sick John Batman was not a fit leader. Coltish was to deliver the sheep to Port Phillip but a gale prevented him entering the Heads. During the gale 115 of the 1124 sheep were killed. He was able to persuade Gellibrand that the sheep could be driven overland to Hobsons Bay, so it was agreed that the ship would land them at Sandy Point. This change of plan was to prove disastrous.

Then Captain Coltish decided instead to land the sheep on Phillip Island and Gellibrand agreed. During the morning of 25 January the sheep were landed at Rhyll by small boats. By noon the surviving 1009 had all been landed but by nightfall the three shepherds could only find 800. That night the shepherds moved the sheep as close as possible to the anchored *Norval* to seek protection against any Aborigines who might be about. This was against Gellibrand's orders.

Many of the thirsty sheep drank salt water and by morning another 280 were dead and the flock was again scattered all over Phillip Island. It was then decided that Mudie and the other shepherds would try to gather all the sheep near the old settlement and that Gellibrand would take a party overland to the Yarra to fetch help.

The day was hot and sultry so the party waited until there was an evening breeze off the water before they slipped across the bay in a small boat from the *Norval*. At about 5 p.m. their boat went ashore on a small sandbar nearly two kilometres from Sandy Point and the eight men aboard had to wait for the morning tide to float it off. They had left with only one water bottle each though it was the middle of summer; also they had a very limited knowledge of the land.

By 6 a.m. on the morning of 28 January they were ashore, almost immediately finding the tracks of a large party of Aborigines. All the men were armed, except Gellibrand, who was too weak to carry a pack or a weapon, so the Aborigines were not regarded as a threat. The real threat, though the party did not realise it, was the heat. By midday, Gellibrand was overcome with the heat. The party halted to wait for him to recover and at least one member drank the last of his water at this stage. Ignoring the danger of becoming lost, he went into the bush to look for more.

The sun was blazing down and the Peninsula was in the grip of a fierce drought. Leake, the man looking for the water, found a small camp of natives with a small soak protected from the sun by bushes. He fetched the rest of the party and they built a shelter of blankets to keep off the worst of the heat. In the evening they moved off again, refreshed and with a new supply of water, hoping to reach Port Phillip by nightfall. At 10 p.m. they halted, still deep in the scrub and too tired to light a fire or cook a meal.

Next morning was as hot as the past few days had been. The party did not bother with breakfast and moved off, still short of water. Soon they realised that they were heading too far to the north and turned more to the west. They found a small saltwater creek which led them out onto the beach near Dromana at about 8 p.m. The heat was still intense but the northerly wind had swung around and great, black clouds were boiling up into the western sky. The bay was tossing and becoming rough.

After half-an-hour's rest they walked on about eight kilometres and found a creek which offered a good supply of fresh water, where they refilled their water bottles and rested again. The party was near where Mornington now stands when the rain began. At first it was a welcome relief from the heat but eventually it grew so heavy that the men were forced to shelter under a blanket-tent, and were now thoroughly miserable and cold.

The rain continued until 2 a.m. but the morning was dry, with a chill wind off the sea. The party measured out its water evenly and then moved off. Here, tragedy very nearly struck. Some way north of

Frankston the party moved inland to higher ground, thinking they were near the Yarra. At noon Gellibrand and young Leake lay down and declared that they could go no further. They were urged to make another effort and struggled down to the beach again. There they found water — a litre each.

At 4 p.m. they were able to continue and by dark they were near what is now Brighton. They found a bark-stripper's hut and the wheelmarks of a cart, so they knew they were at last nearing the settlement. They spent the last night of their terrible march huddled under rain-soaked blankets. Next morning, 31 January, they continued along the beach until at last they came upon the mouth of the Yarra. Gellibrand again collapsed. Four men went up the river toward the settlement and help and soon a boat came down to pick up the remainder of the party. The ordeal was over.

Meanwhile Mudie and his assistants had only collected seventy-eight sheep. This was disaster enough but worse was to come. While Mudie was transferring the sheep, the boat overturned and he and two others were drowned.

Only a year later, Gellibrand and Hesse were dead also, disappearing in fairly mysterious circumstances. Some say that they were speared by the Aborigines in a swamp, others say that Gellibrand was shot by an Aboriginal. All the sources I have discovered suggest that Gellibrand was an experienced bushman and discount the suggestion that he could have become lost and died of thirst or starvation. If his march from Sandy Point was any indication, Gellibrand was not a bushman's bootlace.

It is strange that this tale should have been overlooked by so many historians. While of short duration and of unquestionable foolishness, it was nonetheless an epic walk through unexplored and dry bush in the middle of a heatwave. Gellibrand's wisdom might be questioned, but not his courage.

45 Yannathan

The *Land Act* of 1869 prompted much development on the Koo Wee Rup Swamp. Yannathan was one of the small communities which was born at about this time. It was to take the area only

Top: A typical settler's home 'somewhere in Gippsland'—photographed around 1913.
Photo: Country Roads Board, Victoria.
Bottom: A railway pass to visit the troopship Medic in 1899 (see Story 50)

Top: A view of early Outtrim (see Story 52).
Bottom: Churchill Island from the air (see Story 53).
Photo: Age Suburban Publications

a decade to change dramatically from a black ti-tree swamp to a prosperous farming community.

Early settlers were probably enticed to some extent by the Land Act provision for land rental of one shilling per acre for twenty years. Most came down through Yallock and Grantville, down the swampy and treacherous Western Port Road, some turning off the road and working their way up 'Mac's Lane' to find their 130 hectares. This was the beginning of Yannathan.

Settlement began on the outskirts of Yallock in the early 1870s. By 1880 all the dense forest country had been selected, and clearing and drainage schemes were in full swing. There was no time to be lost. Each farm had to show a return before the limited capital of the selector ran out. There were so many small farmers in the area by 1880 that Yannathan already had two schools, only about three kilometres apart. Apparently there were two sites available and the Education Department, unable to settle the arguments as to which site should be used, eventually built a school on each!

There was never any doubt about the quality of the soil. In fact, the only thing wrong with the soil was that it had too much water mixed in with it! Drainage was important. Every year the Lang Lang River ran over its banks and flooded the swamp for kilometres on either side. Another problem was that there was so little natural drainage that rainwater tended to lie on the surface for weeks on end.

Two comments by pioneers give some idea of what life in Yannathan was like in those days. Mary Ellen Patullo, who later became Mrs Gardiner, said: 'In the year 1877 ... Father selected 300 acres at Lang Lang East, about six miles from Yannathan. It was hilly and heavily timbered. Father cleared half an acre of land and on it erected two rooms, to which two more were added later. So dense was the scrub that the sun could only be seen when directly overhead.'

That comment was made at the Pioneer's Day organised by the Country Women's Association's Yannathan Branch. On the same occasion another speaker, Mrs Rogers, said: 'We passed a man and his wife living in a hut amongst the ti-tree and drove through the gate to a house in the distance. The house was queer. A structure made of ti-tree and bags. No furniture: not a stick was in it except a few homemade stools with legs sprawling everywhere. In the corner of the kitchen was a box pushed into a flour bag and this, if you please, was the safe, and it was here that all the food was kept.'

Soon, however, Yannathan was to become one of Gippsland's most reliable and profitable farming areas. One of the things which caused this was the simple, stubborn courage of the farmers who came to the area. Many of them were Scots who had arrived to make farms for themselves and if this involved great toil and hardship, then so be it.

Early settlers included the Smethursts (whose great numbers led to a suggestion that Yannathan should be renamed Smethurst-borough), the Edeys, the Greaves, Leamons, Wildings, Camerons, Bindings, Kerrs and Murphys. No area on the swamp would be complete without a Murphy! James Smethurst selected 'Bell Bird', opposite the Yannathan school; John Henry Smethurst chose 'Glen Avis' in 1879. James Smethurst Junior selected alongside 'Glen Avis' and the other two sons, Joseph and Samuel, established 'Ferndale' .

The Gardiners were another fairly numerous clan. Robert George Gardiner selected in Yannathan in 1879. Like everyone else, he was a farmer, producing cream and butter for the Melbourne market. To all these farmers the coming of the railway to Lang Lang in 1889 made a great difference. (The official opening was not until 11 November 1890, but the line was in use before that.)

The farmers were, like most, fairly versatile. This was partly because each community had to provide most of its own needs. Grazing was tried and was reasonably successful. The soil was too wet for sheep. Various crops were grown profitably and some vegetables were sold, while bee-keeping was a good sideline for a few.

John Ridgeway made his selection in 1877, on the Lang Lang side of Yannathan. Then Benjamin Lineham came from Clyde in the 1890s to found what almost amounted to a dynasty. His wife had this to say: 'It was covered in high ti-tree and was very wet. The timber for the house had to be carted in from the Monomeith railway station and owing to the bad state of the track it was a long and slow job … We left Cardinia at 9 o'clock in the morning, came as far as the Yallock Creek, where we fed and watered the cows, and then came on, and we were in our new home at 5 in the evening … At this time we got 6d a pound for butter, milk 6d a gallon, and 4d a dozen for eggs.'

Samuel Glover came from Wollert in 1889 and his son, William, became a familiar figure behind his bullock-team. William and

Francis McCraw came from Berwick, where William McCraw had been a butcher.

Yannathan has never thrived in the way that Lang Lang and Cranbourne have done, but it has still been in a very real sense a community. It was very soundly based, with its early settlers mostly Anglicans, hard-headed men who had never been tenant farmers and who understood that the only way to get ahead was by hard work, and plenty of it. They were not highly educated, were typically financially sound but not rich. They were simply interested in building up good farms for the betterment of themselves and their families.

That is why Yannathan went from dismal swamp land in 1880 to excellent farming land by the turn of the century.

46 The Memories Linger On ... St Joseph's, Cora Lynn

Nearly eighty years of service have come to an end for St Joseph's School, Cora Lynn. The stories told of the Sisters of St Joseph and their pupils at Cora Lynn are such, however, that memories of the school will be a long time dying.

Father Keenan, the parish priest at Iona, was approached in 1917 by Mr M. Cunningham and Mr M. Scanlon, with the request that he approve the building of a convent school. The two men had done their homework very thoroughly and had already secured the promise of a block of land, donated by Pat Nestor, if the priest's approval was obtained. When Father Keenan agreed, a 'Queen' carnival was held and most of the money was found immediately. The school was now a certainty and building began almost immediately.

On Trinity Sunday, 1918, the Archbishop of Melbourne, Dr Mannix, arrived to officially open the school. This was a gala event in what was then, and still is, a predominantly Catholic community, with parishioners coming long distances to be present. Dr Mannix took the train to Pakenham and was met by Norman Webster, then only twenty-six years old, who drove him in a buggy over almost impossible roads to the school. The buggy was led by a girl in the costume of an Irish colleen, mounted on a white horse. The 'colleen' was Myrtle Brownhill, later to be Mrs Mead of Gardenvale. On his return, Dr Mannix stayed overnight at Bourke's Hotel under the care of licencee Frank Toll.

The Sisters who taught in the school at Cora Lynn lived in the convent at Iona and were driven to the school each day by Father Keenan and Jack O'Leary; later on Mr Walsh and Mr Scanlon shared the task in their smart new T-model Fords. Eventually a small convent was built behind the school and the daily travelling became unnecessary. When the convent was burnt down in 1938 (much to the disappointment of the local children who hoped that the smoke was coming from the school itself), the Sisters returned to the Iona convent and a daily circuit was arranged from Iona, dropping off teachers at Cora Lynn and Koo Wee Rup.

The driving of Sister Mildred became a legend during this period. Nothing was allowed to stand in her way or to lessen her haste to see the children of Koo Wee Rup and save them from the dread perils of profanity and illiteracy. Her escapes from disaster became notorious in the community and there was at least a suggestion of divine intervention in her driving. She now lives in an infirmary in Havelock Road, Hawthorn, living out the end of a life of service.

Another Sister long remembered is Sister Sylvester. Many of her pupils lived in dread (and some still do) of becoming her 'first failure'. Only 152 centimetres tall, she was the terror of many a strapping 'Grade Sixer'. No-one ever knew what terrible fate awaited her 'first failure' and no-one was at all anxious to find out. Despite the fear she inspired she was also much respected and the students she taught collected a great many scholarships and a great many Merit Certificates, then the ultimate in rural primary education. Sister Sylvester is now the Principal of a much larger school, St Joseph's, Fitzroy.

Sister Augustine was Principal when the school reached an enrolment of seventy. She taught classes up to Intermediate level to save parents the cost of sending their children away to boarding schools. The school provided the 'Josephites' with five recruits between 1922 and 1926 — Veronica Finnegan, Jean Cunningham, Maxcentia Cunningham, Frances Scanlon and Honorius Close.

The dedication of these Sisters and the Order they served is shown by the appalling conditions under which they worked and achieved good results. How many teachers today would be willing to work in one classroom containing eight classes and with only a revolving blackboard as a partition? And how many would be able to achieve the same results?

At this time the parish priest was Father Leo Hartnett, an active man who found time to take some classes at the school and who played football with the Iona and Nar Nar Goon teams.

The corner near the school became another tradition, but one of a very different sort. It was here that the disputes of the day were settled, with even the girls being known to swing a punch or two. A past pupil, Michael Egan, remembers having received a hiding five nights a week from one Tynong lad. His mother eventually took to escorting him home to keep him in one piece. Another fight long remembered was between two girls who battled it out in long-legged navy-blue bloomers, but the fight was not really a fair one. Geraldine had been raised with a family of boys and had learnt the art of self-defence at an early age.

On Sunday, 1 September 1968, St Joseph's School, Cora Lynn, celebrated its jubilee with an outdoor Mass in the schoolyard. The original procession with Dr Mannix was re-enacted, with Mary Bourke playing the part of the colleen. She was accompanied by another lass on horseback and there were three jinkers and a number of vintage cars travelling behind her. Many of the nuns who had taught at the school were present and so was Father Hartnett; the Mass was celebrated by Father Pat Crudden, a past pupil. Other ex-pupils. came from Wagga, Cobram, Adelaide, Nagambie, Tatura, Heyfield and Albury, and all the visitors went home with the locals for tea, afterwards coming back to a dance in Keast Hall.

It is fitting that in the jubilee year of the school the first children of the third generation should have been enrolled. They were Brendan Cunningham and John Cole, and they were the first of many. The name 'Cunningham' is a frequently recurring one. In the first class of twenty-six children, no fewer than fifteen were first cousins of the Cunningham-Scanlon clan. That first class consisted of Agnes, Matthew, John, Vincent, Daniel and Brigid Cunningham, Agnes Rigney, Mary, John and Shiela Scanlon, Peter, Eileen and Sheila Walsh, Eleanor, Thomas, Margaret and Edith Cunningham, Matthew O'Brien, Winifred Tierney, Kevin Fahey, Henry Dineen, Mary and Timothy McGrath, Irene Hart, Brigid Lenane and Thomas Kennedy.

47 The Lights of Cobb and Co!

Through stringy-bark and blue-gum, and box and pine
we go;
A hundred miles shall see to-night the lights of Cobb and
Co.!

When Henry Lawson wrote these lines he was not thinking of Gippsland but he might as well have been. The coach road into Gippsland became one of the most important routes in Australia. Mail and supplies for the growing province were brought up from Melbourne. The return cargo included mail for families far away, survey maps and the precious gold from the Gippsland hills. The coaches brought miners, farmers, ministers, teachers, doctors and all the rag-tag and bobtail of a booming population. They united families and separated them. They brought the good news and the bad, and they were always the fastest link with the outside world.

All along the way inns and hostelries were established to provide food and drink for the travellers and the frequent changes of horses that let Cobb and Co coaches maintain fast schedules in places where the road was little more than a muddy space between the trees. Many of these early buildings still stand today and still serve the public. The traveller between Warragul and Dandenong may, in several places, stand and drink where the driver of the 'Royal Mail' stood a hundred years ago.

The first of the coaching hotels along the way was at Beaconsfield long before there was a regular coach service. The mailman passed through once a week, bound for Alberton, and the only other visitors were bullockies after timber, prospectors after gold, farmers looking for land and the police looking for other people. The Bowman family built their Gippsland Hotel at the main Cardinia Creek crossing, then part of the Panty Gurn Gurn run.

It was licenced in the early 1850s, by which time a small town was beginning to grow up around the crossing. By 1860 it had passed from Bowmans to Souters and had become a substantial collection of buildings. Two things added to the fame of the hotel. The first was its use by Prince Alfred, Duke of Edinburgh, the second son of Queen Victoria, as his residence during an official visit to Victoria in 1869. The Government built two extra rooms on the hotel at no cost to the owners. The second item of fame was its use of extensive stabling for the coach horses, a building which survived until about 1950. This hotel was the first staging point east of Dandenong.

At Pakenham the blown and sweating horses would be changed for a fresh team at the Toomuc Creek and then the next change would be at Bunyip. The gluepots between Bunyip and Picnic Point Hill, and the steep hill itself, meant that another change was necessary at the Robin Hood Hotel, Whisky Creek. This was built by Henry Dickens in 1870. Fresh horses at Brandy Creek and Shady Creek meant that six teams of horses were used to cover a horror stretch fifty-five kilometres long, nearly all of it at breakneck speed. This was how Cobb and Co could reach Sale from Melbourne in only twenty-two hours. There was no real settlement between Berwick and Sale and the road was a long, thin nightmare.

Robert Bain's Border Hotel at Berwick was rarely used by coaches simply because it meant a stop at the bottom of a steep hill and the drivers wanted to keep up their momentum. (Berwick has the same problem, in a different context, today). The Border Hotel was licenced in 1857. The name may have come from the idea then current that that Cardinia Creek marked the 'border' of Gippsland. The first section built was the triangular section on the western side which now houses the public bar. The two storey extension was built at about the time the railway came through, or just before; we might accept 1875 as the approximate date. Mrs Bain added further extensions in a rather ramshackle way after her husband died in 1887.

The Cardinia Creek bridge was built in 1857. Tenders were called on 11 November 1856, with eleven tenderers submitting prices ranging from £600 to £1,240. Needless to say the lowest tenderer secured the contract though his name, Falls, may not have seemed a very good omen.

In 1858 it had become quite obvious that a good road into Gippsland was essential. There were already a number of farming communities on the Gippsland Lakes, supplied by the 'mosquito fleet'. The entrance to the lakes was not always dependable and shipping was becoming very expensive, so the Government accepted the need for such a road and set aside £30,000 for the construction of the Melbourne to Bunyip section. Contractors Cox and Bennett took on the job and began work opposite the Star Hotel in Windsor. Reports at the time and the standard of the road since testify to the excellent quality of their work.

The road was actually being upgraded before the coaches began their operations. In 1856 the first coach service began running to Berwick, there being six coaches weekly between Berwick and Melbourne. Three of these went on to Sale, then still known to most people as Flooding Creek.

There were many other inns and hostelries helping to make the road a hospitable place, such as those at the Cannibal Creek and at Buneep, but one final note provides a small mystery. The Mornington Hotel seems to have become some sort of Flying Dutchman of the hotel trade. Some reports place it at Narre Warren. Some place it north of Mornington and other say it was at Cranbourne. One report even places it at Somerville! This is one area of doubt which waits on the information of those who know of it.

48 Maggie McKinnon's Township

Maggie McKinnon's childhood sweetheart remembered her years later and half a world away. Angus McMillan is said to have named Glenmaggie after her. It was then just a cattle run but it has since become a pleasant little township, well-known to tourists and fishermen and the home of the Glenmaggie Weir and the associated irrigation scheme.

There is another story about the origin of the name which is no less romantic. It is said that when the settlers were considering a name for the new township one old shepherd said that he had once had a very dear girlfriend in Scotland called Maggie Glenn. He suggested reversing her name. We shall probably never know the truth and I suppose it doesn't really matter very much, after all.

The Glenmaggie story begins, not with Angus McMillan, but with Malcolm MacFarlane. He came out to Australia as a young man aged twenty-three, landing in Sydney in 1838. Angus McMillan was his cabin-mate on the voyage and the two men seem to have maintained their friendship for many years. They next met, as far as we know, at Port Albert in 1841.

McMillan was then working for MacAlister and his task was to find a suitable southern outlet from which cattle could be shipped to the Tasmanian market. McMillan and MacAlister both had runs on the 'Maneroo' (the Monaro) and wanted to save the expense of driving their cattle to Sydney for shipping. MacFarlane was one of a group of settlers attracted to Port Albert by reports of good grazing land there. These reports had been made by the survivors of the wreck of the *Clonmel*, which went aground off Port Albert in 1841.

A company called the Port Albert Company was formed to take out and develop the land in the area; they arrived aboard the *Singapore* late in 1841. MacFarlane later led a party from the settlement they established north to the hills and then west to Dandenong. This took them six weeks, and it added greatly to the knowledge of Gippsland held by the public.

In Melbourne the party met the famous William Pearson of Kilmany Park and Walhalla, who took MacFarlane with him to Omeo to buy cattle for Kilmany Park and for MacFarlane's new run at Heyfield. MacFarlane chose the name Heyfield because when he first found the area the grass was as high as his horses' withers.

The Heyfield run was taken up by Malcolm MacFarlane for James MacFarlane. Malcolm managed it for fifteen years during which time he found the Glenmaggie area and took up the land in his own name. Malcolm died on 13 October 1899, at the ripe old age of eighty-nine. He was buried at Glenmaggie and there are descendants of his there today. His wife, Flora, died on 26 June 1904, aged seventy-one.

In about 1860 the first selectors began to move into the Glenmaggie area, taking up land under the Duffy Act, which allowed them thirty-two hectares of land under a conditional purchase system. Under this system, a rent of one shilling per acre was paid annually and, subject to sufficient improvements being made, a grant of the land was made after twenty years. This was eventually altered to allow the selector 130 hectares as it had become obvious that in most places thirty-two hectares was simply not enough. Before the selectors were allowed to claim land, however, the original 'squatter' was allowed to choose 260 hectares as a pre-emptive right.

Names listed among the earliest settlers include MacFarlane, Cummings, Fullerton, Marshall, Henderson, Molphy, Chester, Timms, Monds, Green and Garvey. Some of these names are still prominent in the district.

The first Glenmaggie school was probably a private school operated on MacFarlane's property but the details are unclear. We know, however, that the first official school was No. 1576, Glenmaggie, opened on 22 June 1875. This school was called the Gower Creek Bridge State School. Glenmaggie Creek was originally Gower Creek and the bridge became known as Gleesons Bridge.

The first Head Teacher was Miss Clara Weekes, sister-in-law of Henry Tisdall, the Head Teacher at Walhalla. The Tisdalls have recently been very well-publicised for their role in Victorian education. The school was not shifted when the weir was first built but it became necessary to move it in 1957 when the weir was extended. The original building was demolished but the pine trees which surrounded it are still visible.

There was once a school at Seaton, then called Bald Hills, which was opened as a private school in January 1866, but which apparently lasted only a short time. Seaton State School, No. 1649, opened on 1 January 1876 and finally closed on 26 September 1944, though it had been closed between 1927 and 1933. There was also another school which was known for a time as the Glenmaggie school. This was Gravel Hill, No. 1949. It was also called Glenmaggie North and had a chequered history, being burnt down, rebuilt, closed and eventually (in 1925) being taken away to Airly on a bullock dray.

A school of an even more temporary nature was Glenmaggie Weir State School, No. 4046. This school was near the weir and was built solely to serve the children of the construction workers. It was opened on 1 February 1921, and closed in December 1928.

The weir itself was commenced in 1919 in response to pressure from farmers on the flats of the Macalister River, who needed irrigation for their maize, sugar beet, lucerne and fodder crops. The first deliveries of water were in the Boisdale area in 1925.

During the early 1920s the weir slowly filled and the original Glenmaggie township, or a large part of it, was gradually submerged.

On 9 May 1929, the *Maffra Spectator* carried a story about a petition signed by fifty-two local residents expressing displeasure with the decision to build the new town on the north side of the township bridge. They wanted the new town on the south side, nearer to the railways and the markets. The Maffra Shire Council agreed that the people who paid the rates in the area should have the main say and the town was rebuilt on the south side, as the locals wanted it.

In 1927-28 the weir was filled to capacity but it was soon obvious that it could not meet the demand for irrigation water in the area, although the weir was not extended until 1957, when new irrigation areas were opened at North Newry, West Boisdale, Montgomery, The Heart (near Sale) and near Heyfield. This extension caused the school to be shifted again.

Glenmaggie is, obviously enough, a pleasant place in which to live or to holiday but it has seen its share of hard times. There were large floods in 1891, two in 1911, 1916, 1925 and 1935. There have been several bushfires, notably in 1926 and 1965, and there have been a number of serious droughts. One of these was in 1938 and another was in 1972-3.

Still, these little settlements are in many ways the backbone of Gippsland and they have learned to handle their own problems over the years. The people of Glenmaggie are of pioneer stock and their town will survive.

49 Walhalla Boatmen

Can you imagine building a boat at Walhalla? Can you imagine boating on the rock-strewn Thompson River? That it is possible can be discovered by reading a small booklet entitled 'Walhalla Boatmen', taken from the notes of Henry Tisdall, which was published to raise funds for the now-defunct Walhalla school. The booklet tells a hair-raising tale of the lengths to which some fishermen will go.

Henry Thomas Tisdall, Captain George Standish Hartrick, John Herbert Langhorne and, probably, Hubert Florance are the star players in the adventure. There was a large pool in the river where they often thought they could catch good fish if only they could get out to the middle. The obvious answer was a boat and the men set to work to build one. The man in charge of the project was Captain Hartrick.

Like the sailors in the popular cartoon, though, the men came up with an old problem. The boat was soon built but the shed in which they built it was a long way from the water. Tisdall wrote: 'Here was a puzzle. She weighed over a quarter of a ton and there was an immense hill between us and the desired haven, with no road of any description; on the contrary, there was nothing but primeval forest.' Remember that all this took place in the 1880s when Walhalla had not long risen to national fame as a deep-lead gold mining town.

Florance had an idea. Why not put the boat on a dray? It could then be taken out along the Toongabbie Road to the Thompson River bridge, about thirteen kilometres away. There it could be lowered into the water and the four would-be fishermen could sail it, or her, back up the river as best they could. The boat had a mast and sails but the oars were probably a great deal more use.

A number of local residents followed the dray down to the river and helped with the launching. It isn't hard to imagine that some of the comments may well have been rather ribald. The four sailors jumped in and began to pull on the oars with great vigour. After ten minutes they had made no headway and there was a good deal of laughter from the spectators on the bank. On that first day they managed to travel only one kilometre or so before darkness caught up with them. In the deep valleys around Walhalla the sun is late to rise and early to set.

After a good meal and a few well-told jokes around the fire, and some very successful fishing, our four heroes bedded down, only to find that morning seemed to be upon them almost instantly. The second day saw them repeating the process of manhandling the boat through the rapids and then rowing along the deep pools that lay between. During the day they came to one area where the miners had narrowed the river to a third of its original width by making a long dam. This left much of the riverbed dry and made it much easier to sluice the gravel and pan out the gold. This obstruction was not overcome until midday and the men then spent some time watching the miners at work. That night they sheltered from heavy rain in a tent made from the sails and the oars. This was erected over the boat, in which they slept.

The third day was marred by a near-disaster. In the morning they came to a place where the river was divided into two narrow races by a rocky outcrop. They got the boat in under the outcrop but they could not make any headway against the fierce current on either side. Hubert Florance took a rope ashore, making the crossing balanced precariously on a narrow and rotten log. He attached the rope to the base of a large tree above the rapids and the men were able to haul the boat up against the current hand over hand. Progress was painfully slow and the boat was nearly lost several times.

This brought them to another large pool along which they rowed merrily enough. At the far end, though, the pool shallowed and they had to make a channel by lifting out the rocks. This was hard, cold and slow work. It was nearly dark when they reached the next pool and there they discovered that the boat was badly sprung and was taking water very quickly. The main leak had apparently been caused by a knock from a large rock but there were other leaks along the seams and joints. They covered the main leak with Tisdall's coat and rowed desperately for the shore. That night there was no fishing. It was nearly midnight before the boat was repaired.

On the fourth day, provisions began to run out, as the men had planned to spend only a couple of days on the journey. In the afternoon they came to what was virtually a waterfall. This was obviously going to take some time to negotiate and the only supplies left were two bottles of beer and some fish. They decided to return to the township on foot but even this was to prove a difficult task.

Walhalla (Stringers Creek) was sixteen kilometres away, and it was a very rugged distance. One beer bottle was divided to give the men the energy to start walking. The second was divided half-way up the hill to give them the strength to keep going. Eventually they made the town, where they spent two days recuperating.

After their two days the men returned to the task. Three days saw them at Coppermine (Coopers Creek) where the miners turned out in force to watch them. They could not believe that anyone would try to bring a boat up the Thompson River — and I find it hard to believe myself.

The next stage of the river was very shallow and the boat was hauled along by ropes. The main problem with this was that the flat rocks in the riverbed were very slippery and the two men pulling at any given time often slipped and disappeared beneath the water. This was a source of much amusement to ex-sailor Hartrick who stayed in the boat to steer it.

Just before sunset on the third day (actually the seventh day of travelling) they came at last to the large dam which held back the pool which had inspired them in the first place. Here there was another problem. The boat had to be raised to the top of the dam to launch it. Hartrick directed the operation and, when the boat was perched atop the rock wall, ordered the others to stand back while he pushed the boat into the water. Much to his discomfiture he followed it into the pool and the others, at whose expense he had enjoyed a number of laughs during the afternoon could only roll about on the bank, howling with completely undignified laughter.

Unfortunately the booklet does not tell us whether the men caught many fish in the big pool. Still, anyone who knows the Thompson River will know what a Herculean effort it must have been to move a boat upstream along it. If the boat, or its remains, could be found they would make an interesting addition to the tourist attractions of what is already a fascinating place.

50 The 'Gippsland Bushrangers'

The 52nd Battalion was the Gippsland Regiment. It was also known less reverently as 'The Gippsland Bushrangers'. The Gippsland Regiment was originally part of the Victorian Rangers so bushrangers' might not be an inappropriate word. It was then called the Gippsland Battalion and covered the area between Port Phillip and Rosedale. The unit was unique in that, though it was an infantry unit, it sent more mounted men to the Boer War than did any other formation. The first Victorian officer killed in South Africa was Major Eddy, a member of the unit.

It is believed that the first Victoria Cross awarded to a Victorian went to a member of the Gippsland Battalion of the Victorian Rangers. It is also said that King Edward VII presented the Victorian Rangers with special colours, a singular honour. After the South African War and before the First World War the Gippsland

Battalion was disbanded and its members formed the nuclei of the 13th Battalion Light Horse and the Gippsland Infantry Regiment. One company, the Peninsular Company, was later used as the basis of the 46th Battalion.

After the evacuation of Gallipoli the 52nd Regiment was raised. This was to become a 'Gippsland' regiment though it had very few Victorians and a great many Queenslanders when it was first raised. This unit because part of the 4th Division and fought with distinction in France. The unit colours carry the Battle Honours awarded during this period. In 1918 the 52nd became the 2nd Battalion, 5th Australian Infantry Regiment. It was 1922 before it again became the 52nd Battalion, the Gippsland Regiment.

The Commanding Officer of the new Gippsland Regiment was Lieutenant-Colonel Knox, later to become Brigadier Sir George Knox. He was in charge of the regiment when compulsory military training was reintroduced. Knox had replaced Major R. Cox, the first officer appointed to the new regiment. The headquarters were at Dandenong and men were recruited from as far west as Caulfield and as far east as the border. Once again, Gippsland had its own regiment.

In 1925, while Knox was Commanding Officer, the unit was presented with its new colours at a very impressive ceremony in the Dandenong Showgrounds. The 'new' 52nd Battalion, C.M.F., carried on the proud tradition of the 52nd Battalion, A.I.F. Lord Somers was invited to become Honorary Colonel of the regiment when he became Governor of Victoria. He accepted and filled this post from 1927 to 1930.

Nor was this merely a 'paper' appointment. Lord Somers visited the regiment frequently and often accompanied it on camps and exercises. Perhaps because of this appointment, the 52nd Battalion twice had the privilege of forming the Guard of Honour at the opening of State Parliament and they filled the same role on the wharf when Lord Somers left Victoria. Their colours were also paraded every Anzac Day but there were usually very few men marching behind them because so many of the 52nd's 'Anzacs' came originally from other States.

There was a cutback in military spending in the 1930s and the 52nd was amalgamated with the 37th to become the 37/52nd Battalion, part of the 10th Brigade. Before the Second World War there was a boost in recruiting for the militia and it was decided that the 52nd should again become a separate unit. Again the headquarters were at Dandenong and there were training centres at Oakleigh, Dandenong, Garfield, Pakenham, Catani, Warragul and Yallourn. These were soon followed by new depots at Sale, Maffra, Traralgon and Bairnsdale.

By the end of 1938 the battalion was over 1600 strong, perhaps the largest militia unit this country has ever seen. There were so many men that the annual camp had to be conducted in two parts; eventually it was decided to split, the unit in two. The part that stayed as the 52nd Division remained in the Dandenong headquarters and served the area between Oakleigh and Warragul.

Early in 1940 the unit was built up with National Service trainees and training became, naturally enough, much more intense. Full mobilisation of the 52nd took place in 1941. The battalion moved to Queensland to prepare for a confrontation with the Japanese but while they were training the 6th and 7th Divisions returned from the Middle East and the Australian forces were regrouped. The 52nd again became the 37/52nd though many men were lost to other units.

The 37/52nd saw active service in the islands and did nothing to blemish the proud record of the regiment. Men of the 52nd were spread far and wide during the war. Some even served with the R.A.N. and R.A.A.F. Two famous Australian soldiers had the 52nd under their commands during the war. Field Marshall Sir Thomas Blamey commanded the 10th Brigade and the 3rd Division when they included the 52nd, and Lieutenant-General Sir Stanley Savige also commanded the 10th Brigade, from 1936 until the mobilisation.

In 1942, when the 52nd Battalion, the Gippsland Regiment, ceased to exist as a separate unit, the then Commanding Officer, Lieutenant-Colonel A. Symons, returned the colours to Dandenong. They were last paraded in Queensland before this and, happily, many of the Queenslanders who had helped to earn the Battle Honours on the colours were there for the parade. The colours were handed over to the trustees of the St James Church of England in Dandenong for safekeeping. They were back in the town where the battalion had been headquartered for so many years.

On 26 September 1954, the colours were handed over to Brigadier Sir George Knox and Mr Norm Duell from the 52nd

Top: The Royal Hotel, Koo Wee Rup, opened in 1915 (see Story 57).
Bottom: The arrival of the first train to Walhalla on 15 March 1910 (see Story 55)

Top: 'Harewood' homestead, once a social centre for the area north of Western Port (see Story 60). Bottom: An early engine on the Mirboo Line, photographed in 1887 (see Story 62)

Battalion (Gippsland Regiment) Association. These two gentlemen then transferred the colours to the Shrine of Remembrance for permanent safekeeping. They were placed in the Shrine on 5 December 1954.

Now the Gippsland area has another regiment headquartered in Dandenong, the 2/15th Field Regiment of the Royal Regiment of Australian Artillery. This was once called the City of Dandenong and Gippsland Regiment.

The depots once used by the infantry-cum-cavalry of the 52nd Battalion are now used by artillery, engineering and armoured units. The Prince of Wales Light Horse units in Central Gippsland perhaps have the best claim to being the true descendants of the 52nd and the Gippsland Battalion of the Victorian Rangers. In any case, it is safe to say the original spirit is still alive today.

51 Tarra Algon, River of Little Fish

In 1841 six men from the Port Albert Company decided to walk back to Melbourne in the hope of finding good land along the way. They were W. A. Brodribb, Alex Kinghorne, Kirsopp, McLeod, McFarlane and Charlie Tarra, who had been Strzelecki's guide. At about the same time three other men left Melbourne headed east to see if it was possible to drive cattle into Gippsland. This second party consisted of Albert Brodribb, Edward Barker and Edward Hobson. The two parties were to reshape our knowledge of Gippsland.

The first party crossed the same river as Strzelecki had mentioned. They crossed the Latrobe near where he had crossed it and then headed west along the foothills. They crossed the Tyers River, which they called the Kinghorne, and the Morwell River, which they showed on their chart as the Kirsopp.

The second party reached the port but did so with very great difficulty. They returned to Melbourne along the coast and found the going somewhat better, a fact which led to the coastal route into Gippsland being preferred for some years. This was the route Edward Hobson used when he took cattle into Gippsland to take up the run his brother had been granted on the Morwell River. Edward was the younger brother of Edmund Hobson. Edmund was a surgeon of some note and Edward managed his farming interests more or less as a partner. Edward chose a location on the Morwell River where the city of Traralgon now stands and it may be said that this marked the end of the exploration period in Gippsland and the beginning of the settlement phase.

It was the Hobsons who chose the name 'Tarra Algon', meaning 'river of little fish', for the area. They never spelt the name in any consistent way themselves. At times it appeared as 'Tralgon' and then 'Traralgon.'

Other settlers soon appeared. William Bennett, with the help of Hugh Reoch and Albert Brodribb, found reasonable grazing in the vicinity of what is now Hazelwood, or Churchill. Thomas Gorringe took up land between the Hobsons and Bennett, calling his run Mary Ville. John Fowler Turnbull gave up his store at Port Albert and took up land near Flooding Creek (Sale) and then at Loy Yang. Later he was to become one of Traralgon's leading citizens.

In November, 1845, a party of Native Police from the Narre Warren Depot cut a track through from Traralgon. This proved to be a much better route than the 'road' along the coast so the police patrols used it regularly and they became a form of unofficial mail service for the settlers. Money for the Port Albert traders was also carried by the police. The road improved slowly but when Malcolm Campbell found a navigable entrance to the Gippsland Lakes, there seemed to be less need for a road than there was before and little was done in the way of improvements.

The Traralgon township was first surveyed in 1848. There were only two buildings, Hobson's and Winsor's, on the maps they drew but they did mark out and name Kay Street, the only street. A second survey carried out in 1858 resulted in the marking out and naming of Franklin, Grey, Seymour and Hotham Streets. On these maps the name 'Taralgon' appears, which, while the spelling is incorrect, indicates the first official use of the name.

In this year coach services became fairly regular and this persuaded Duncan Campbell to build the Traveller's Rest Hotel. Peter Smith already ran a grog shanty but the elaborate new building, with fourteen bedrooms, meant that the shanty licence was not renewed and the already-affluent Campbell forced Smith out of business.

The first Traralgon land sale was held at Sale on 29 August 1859. The police magistrate, Captain Carey, sold most of the blocks to none other than Duncan Campbell. With the discovery of gold in the hills in 1859 the number of travellers increased greatly and Campbell became a very rich man indeed.

In 1859 the Governor approved the town boundaries shown in the second survey and the name 'Traralgon' was officially fixed. The small village grew steadily, the first policeman being appointed in 1860. He was Constable John O'Connor and his 'beat' extended west to the Bunyip River and north to the Baw Baw goldfields. His was the only police station between Sale and Dandenong.

The first post office was opened in January, 1861, and the Postmaster was the ubiquitous Duncan Campbell. In that year Traralgon had a population of thirty-six and there were six buildings within the town boundaries. July 31 of 1861 also saw the first issue of the *Gippsland Times*. Even this was not Traralgon's first newspaper. There had been the *Independent* but it had lasted only a few months. In 1864 the telegraph line passed through Traralgon and the outside world became just that little bit closer, though there was no connection in the town for some time and telegrams could only be sent from Sale.

Traralgon grew steadily but slowly. It did not become a Borough until 1961, one hundred years after the first post office was opened in the town. Yet, only three years later, in April 1964, Sir Rohan Delacombe, Governor of Victoria, declared Traralgon a city. It had come a long way from the Hazelwood, Mary Ville and Tarra Algon runs.

52 Down But Not Out at Outtrim

One of the earliest cattle runs in Gippsland was the Wild Cattle Run, supposedly named for the wild cattle which survived from the short-lived settlement at Corinella. It covered 100,000 hectares and was bounded by the Tarwin River, the Strzelecki Ranges, the sea and a line drawn north from the mouth of the Powlett River. Among the names of the earliest settlers there were Murdock and Donald McLeod, George Matthieson, Dr Birney and a gentleman named Elms.

The area had an another resident but he wasn't a settler in the usual sense. He was Martin Weiberg. This enterprising fellow robbed the mail steamer Avoca in August 1877, making off with 5,000 gold sovereigns consigned by the Oriental Bank.

Weiberg was arrested on suspicion shortly after the crime but he was no fool. He offered to lead the police to the loot and they duly escorted him to the banks of the Tarwin River. There he told them the remainder of the deal he was prepared to make. He would only show one policeman the hiding place. After some hesitation the police agreed that Constable Mahony, a champion runner, would escort Weiberg across the river. Weiberg wasn't really interested in Mahony as an escort. He dealt the policeman a terrific kick in the stomach and disappeared into the bush.

For three years he lived on the shores of Andersons Inlet, using the tides to conceal his tracks. Eventually he was recaptured and sentenced to a long term of imprisonment. On his release he came back to the Inlet and there he is supposed to have drowned. No-one really knows. His boat was found adrift and that was all the evidence that was ever discovered.

In 1893 Arthur Johnson inadvertently wrote a chapter in the history of Outtrim. He was shooting wallabies on a property his father had leased when he found an outcropping of coal. Testing showed that the coal was of excellent quality and Arthur and his brother sank a shaft which showed that the seam was well over one metre thick.

Being inexperienced in the wicked ways of this rather wicked world, the two young men took their samples to one prospector for coal named Bellamy, who worked for the Jeetho Coal Company of Korumburra. Bellamy promptly registered a claim in the name of his company and the boys were left without any legal comeback. Ross McCartney, a major shareholder in the company, promised the boys a share but this promise was apparently never fulfilled.

For some obscure reason the original finder of the coal was later invited to select a new name for the area and he chose 'Outtrim', naming it for the then Minister for Mines, Mr A. R. Outtrim. M.L.A. Johnson reportedly sought compensation for the loss of his find and suspicion was widely felt when his body was later found in the railway cutting opposite the Bridge Hotel on 26 January 1903. His death was never really explained.

The original claim was called the 'Lord Hopetoun', after the Governor-General of the day, before Johnson chose the new name. In July 1894 Murdock McLeod, on whose property the coal had been found, and who had acquired the mineral lease, arranged with R. B. Stamp, a Melbourne estate agent, to form the Outtrim

Company. This was later amalgamated with the Howitt Company.

After more testing work began in earnest. The main shaft was driven within a short distance of the original discovery. Stamp had meanwhile purchased the McLeod selection and divided it into building blocks. Each miner employed had to agree to buy a block for £8. On this he was to build a house and pay it off at 6s per week. The settlements which sprang up around the mine rejoiced in such names as Happy Flat and Mount Pleasant, but there was also the inevitable Mount Misery. The staircase from the railway station side of the bridge to the main business area was called the Golden Staircase and the steps leading down the other side were called the Silver Staircase.

Serious mining began in 1895 with a government contract for 66,000 tons at 9s 6d a ton. The coal was taken by bullock wagon to nearby Jumbunna for rail transport to Melbourne. In January 1896 the railway was extended to Outtrim at a cost of £11,720 per mile. The mining company put up a guarantee of £20,000 and provided all the land for railway use at no cost to the Government.

The mines were then working twenty-four hours daily, the miners working in three shifts. Paid 13s 9d daily, they averaged three and a half tonnes per man per day. Daily output exceeded 500 tonnes. Yearly production was expected to be 66,000 tonnes but in the first full year of operation the mine yielded 126,000 tonnes and the company declared a dividend of £8,700.

In 1898, of the 240,000 tonnes of coal mined in Victoria, Outtrim produced 140,000. Jumbunna produced 70000 and Korumburra managed only 30,000 tonnes. By 1900-1902, when the peak of production was reached, the township of Outtrim was booming, with more than 4,000 residents. There were 400 children at the school, 500 miners, two policemen, five churches, two hotels and a wine saloon. There was an Outtrim Racing Club with its own track on the flats three kilometres from the town, and the Outtrim Cup carried stake money high enough to attract Melbourne horses. In fact, after one meeting in which Melbourne horses won every race, the stake money was lowered so they would not come back!

In 1903 Outtrim fell from the heights of optimism to the depths of the blackest despair. Newcastle colliers cut the prices they charged the Victorian Railways. The miners were faced with drastic wage cuts if Outtrim coal was to remain competitive. At the same time there was an industrial dispute when the company dropped its incentive payments under which a miner could earn up to £3 per day. When the miners refused to work under the new system the company imported what it called 'free labourers'. Immediately, trouble flared.

There were torchlight processions and tar-and-featherings became a commonplace event. The police force was increased to thirty-eight. When the strike was settled in May 1904, after seventy weeks of trouble, everyone was a loser. The miners finished up on about 7s 10d per shift and the company was receiving much lower prices for its coal. Also there had been an exodus during the strike.

In 1910 Outtrim reeled under two more body blows. A large fire damaged the commercial area and then a second fire completed the task. Then coal was discovered at Wonthaggi and the big mine at Outtrim went into liquidation. The exodus became a stampede. Some of the houses were shifted to Inverloch by bullock dray but most were shifted to Wonthaggi.

Today there are only a few tracks, a small school, the mullock heaps and a few brick walls to show where the mine and town once stood. There can be very few substantial towns in Australia that have gone from rags to riches and back again quite so quickly.

53 Churchill Island

The night of 5 January 1798 was wild and stormy. Great rolling waves came out of the west to smash themselves on the uncharted southern shore. The howl of a Bass Strait gale was the only sound that could be heard over the hiss and roar of the water. When George Bass saw the black bulk of what he named Cape Wollomi he knew that he had found shelter. He ran his whaleboat in behind the cape, into the Eastern Passage.

The following morning, Bass realised that he had discovered a large bay with one main island and several smaller islets. He thought that what is now French Island was a part of the mainland to his north. One of the small islets he discovered was later to be named Churchill Island. Now, in 1976, that small island has been purchased by the Victorian Government for a new and much-needed National Park. At a cost of $400,000 a priceless part of our heritage has been preserved.

Bass stayed in Western Port only twelve days but he was fully occupied during that time. He chose the name Western Port, incidentally, because it was then the most westerly of the known harbours in New South Wales. During the twelve days Bass explored the coast of Phillip Island and walked across the eastern end of it. He found fresh water in the Bass River on the mainland.

His report stated that Phillip Island would support a farming settlement though he was certain that he was seeing it at a time of drought. He also reported an abundance of wildfowl and this is reflected in the purchase of the island for the protection of the flora and fauna.

In 1800 Lieutenant James Grant, commanding HMS *Lady Nelson*, passed eastward through Bass Strait, the first navigator to have done so. On reaching Sydney he was sent to make a full exploration of Western Port, as the *Lady Nelson* had been especially fitted-up for survey work before leaving England. Grant was the next white man to see Churchill Island, sighting it on 28 March 1801.

Lieutenant Grant called Churchill Island 'Grant Land' and wrote that he scarcely knew a place he should rather call his own than this little island. He and his sailors planted the seeds of wheat, onions, potatoes, cucumbers, pumpkins, melons, apples, plums, peaches, rice and coffee. Most of these seeds had been given him by John Churchill of Dawlish, Devonshire, England, whose name was eventually given to the island. Though most of the seeds failed, this was the first gardening or agriculture of any kind in what was to become Victoria.

Later in the same year Acting-Lieutenant John Murray, the new commander of the *Lady Nelson*, visited the island. He found a hut Grant had built and he found that the wheat had grown nearly two metres high. This fact was to make a great impression on colonial administrators of the future.

The first permanent resident of Churchill Island was Samuel Pickersgill, who squatted there in 1857. He had no formal title to the land and was displaced by the first legal occupier, John Rogers. Pickersgill had found a cabin of much later vintage than Grant's but to this day no-one knows who built it, or why. After all these years, the name of the builder and his fate have become just one more of the many unsolved mysteries of the coastline.

John Rogers went to live on the island some time in 1866. His title, or lease, was dated on 15 January of that year. He did not stay long for he next appears in the pages of history as the second settler in the Brandy Creek district at some time between 1868 and 1877. While on the island, and later, he was known as a careful and conscientious farmer. Before he came to the Brandy Creek district he conducted correspondence to find out just how well the popular technique of burning the forest and planting seed on the ashes would work. He did not come to Brandy Creek until he was certain this economical system worked well. His 130 hectares at Brandy Creek became such an inspiration to other settlers that the Government awarded him another eighty-one hectares as a form of recognition. His farm became a model for others to follow, and his advice was available to all.

Rogers sold the island to Samuel Amess in either 1872 or 1877, depending on which set of records one trusts. I suspect that it was 1872. The Amess family owned the island until 1921 with three generations holding the title in turn. Samuel Amess had been the Mayor of Melbourne during 1865 and he had played host to the officers of the Confederate States of America's raiding ship *Shenandoah*. This little piece of hospitality was to cost the British Government the huge sum of £850,000 in compensation to the victorious United States of America.

In this hospitality Amess was supported by John Cleeland, owner of the nearby Woolamai run. Cleeland even named one of his racehorses 'Shenandoah' and won the Australian Cup with her, the jockey wearing the Confederate colours of grey and gold. He entertained the crew of the ship at his Albion Hotel in Bourke Street, the departure point for most of the Cobb and Co country coach routes. With another of his horses, Cleeland won the 1875 Melbourne Cup. The horse was Wollamai, bred on the island and ridden by Bob Batty. It took three minutes and thirty-eight seconds to cover the distance. By today's times, he would be entering the straight when the winner was crossing the line but in those days it was good enough to win the Cup.

The Captain of the *Shenandoah* gave Samuel Amess a cannon as a token of appreciation, which Amess took to Churchill Island and a tradition grew up that it be fired every New Year's Eve.

The Amess family sold out to G. N. Buckley in 1921. He died in 1935 and the three executors of his will took over the title. In

1944 they sold it to a Collins Street dentist, Edward Jenkins, who owned it until his death in 1963, leaving it to his nurse in gratitude. Jenkins built the bridge which connects the island to Phillip Island, an undertaking of no mean size.

The last private owners were Nick Thyssen and Alex Classou. They paid $31,0000 for the island at auction but were soon told that the Government was very interested in its purchase. After brief negotiations they were paid $400,000.

The island now belongs, quite properly, to the people of Victoria. All being well it will prove a handsome addition to the system of National Parks and will preserve at least a little of Western Port from the worst depredations of the tourist, the developer and the industrialist.

54 The Bennett Diary

Hazel Bennett was given a diary by her brother on 20 March 1835. The diary William gave her was 'Marshall's Ladies Elegant Pocket Souvenir for 1835'. Neither William nor Hazel knew how important that diary would be in years to come. Nor were they to know that Hazel Bennett would give her name to Hazelwood.

William Bennett came out from Somerset to Van Diemens Land in 1832. There, in 1833, he married Hazel Brodribb, his cousin and the daughter of William Adams Brodribb. Their first child, Kenric, was born in 1836. Lavinia Mary followed in 1837, Frances Emma in 1839, Frederica in 1841, Francis George in 1843, Eliza Adams in 1847, Jane Maria in 1849, Flora Blanche in 1851 and Edward William Charles in 1853.

In 1838 the Bennett family left Van Diemens Land to take up land in South Australia. There they were apparently unsuccessful because in 1844 they began an epic trek into Gippsland, to what was to become the Hazelwood run.

In 1844 Hazel used the diary her brother had given her to record the details of this trek. The diary, a goldmine for historians, was lost until the debate occurred over whether Hazelwood should be renamed in honour of Winston Churchill. The Hazelwood Retention Committee received a letter from New South Wales, from Mrs Ruby Bates of Crows Nest. She pointed out that she was a descendant of the Bennetts. The Morwell Historical Society followed this up and discovered two other descendants. One of these had the diary, a discovery of great significance.

The extracts given here are reproduced in the Morwell Historical Society News, vol. iv (1965), ch. 10. They tell the story much better than I could.

'*21.4.1844*. This morning we left Ballarana in company with Mr Hobson who was taking cattle into Gippsland. The party consisted of himself and three men, ours William, myself and five children, the bullock driver, his wife and child. We made about 11 miles this day ... Next morning we proceeded to the Manton's station, five miles. Here we were joined by Mr Reoch with 300 cattle, Mr — with 50; also three Scotsmen with a dray.

'*24.4.1844*. We made the inlets known by the name of Muddy Creeks about three in the afternoon. With much difficulty the cattle crossed over ... There was not time to cross the drays this evening.

'*25.4.1844*. The men got up early and crossed one dray. The other sunk so deep in mud that they were obliged to leave it until the tide rose, which was not till evening. This prevented us moving any further.

'*26.4.1844*. Rose very early. With great work, whipping, hallooing, and dragging, we succeeded in crossing the other three inlets. Two cows were lost in the bog. We reached Mr Jameson's Station, a distance of three miles. This is called the Head of Western Port. This part of the country is well grassed. The plains are very rich but very wet in the winter season.

'*28.4.1844*. Reached Martin's, four miles from Jameson's. Crossed two rivers, both very boggy. At this place we met Mr Thomas, the black's' protector ... Mr Martin was kind enough to send us some milk and butter which was a great treat.

'*29.4.1844*. Travelled over a great deal of barren, heathy ground. Reached the Hurdee Gurdee Creek in time to get our camp fixed before dark. A most miserable place, surrounded on every side with burnt scrub and old gum trees.

'*30.4.1844*. Expected to get to Massy and Anderson's but owing to the thick scrub and deep creeks we had to pass, did not do so.

The scrubs were dreadful but the creeks much more so, the banks of which were so deep that the bullocks and drays were let down with ropes. We crossed three in this way. Stormy, cold weather which made us very miserable. We travelled till dark and then we missed our road ... We camped in a very wet place, everything wet ...

'1.5.1844. Sent two of the men to look for the cattle track. They soon found it ... we had now a good road through rather a pretty country to Massy and Anderson's ... We had to remain at the station until the 4th for provisions. We camped on the bank of a large river navigable for small vessels ... All the stations in this quarter are cultivation: None of them is stocked in consequence of the great difficulty in getting stock down, the road is so bad. The settlers get all their produce to market by water.

'5.5.1844. Made a very early start, fully determined to get out of the settled districts ... At 12 o'clock we got to the last station, a poor, wretched place, close to the bay. We stayed here till evening as we had a wide inlet to cross and could not do it before the tide fell.

'6.5.1844. ... We reached within one mile of the Tarwin but not till an hour after dark. The children and I had to walk for some miles, the scrub was so frightfully bad. This was very fatiguing; the wheel track of the dray was the only path. We had the greatest trouble to force our way ...

'9.5.1844. We moved down to the Tarwin with the intention of crossing. A fence was made to keep the cattle up and at low tide the cattle were brought to the riverside but, to each one's disappointment, they refused to go into the water. Mr Hobson had them forced and drowned 11 without getting one to go over.

'10.5.1844. ... Mr Hobson and Mr Reoch went up the river to find another crossing place.

Remember that Hazel Bennett had a young family with her during all this and that the party had passed beyond the last station at Inverloch and were now in the completely uninhabited Tarwin valley. On 14 April they camped in a large swamp. There was no wood for a fire and it rained continuously. It was very cold and one of the children had become ill. Mrs Bennett and the children were sharing the one tent with all the men.

'*15.5.1844.* We got over the river and had to walk nearly up to our knees in water for a mile over a reedy swamp. The poor children had great trouble in getting along. I had to carry one some of the way and Bennett another all of the way. The gents and men were employed in dragging with ropes the horses and cattle out of the bog … Most of the cattle were got out and all the horses except one which died in the bog.

'*16.5.1844.* Wet the whole day with occasional hail showers and bitter cold. We were obliged to put ourselves on short allowance of bread.

'*17.5.1844.* With much joy bid farewell to the Tarwin. Did not make more than three miles … over several cold, wet swamps.

'*18.5.1844.* Made an early start over country never before visited by civilised man.

'*19.5.1844.* Wet all day with the wind SW. We camped early. The cattle knocked up for want of food … the bedding quite wet … great fears of our flour running out.

'*20.5.1844.* Delighted with a sight of Corner Inlet, about 20 miles from Port Albert, the capital of Gipps Land, if so it may be called … high, heathy hills and deep creeks, thickly scrubbed. The cattle are getting quite weak for want of grass .

'*21.5.1844.* The creeks were more numerous and more difficult to cross. The drays nearly upset several times; the poor bullocks more than once thrown down. The drayman got into such passions at times I thought he would have killed his bullocks. His wife did not escape his rages. He threatened to — her down as well … many of the cattle were left behind, too weak to travel.

'*23.5.1844.* Mr Hobson left with the black for the Port. He has gone for supplies which he intends to send down by water … The scrub is almost impossible. It is Mr Reoch's opinion that it is impossible to get the cattle in and that they will be compelled to return to Melbourne.

'*24.5.1844.* The men were employed in making a bridge over the creek we were camped on … a yard was put up on the banks. The yard was built … to prevent watching … but no sooner were the cattle put into the yard than lo! and behold! down it came . . .

'*25.5.1844.* The gentlemen were occupied in rebuilding the yard. The men bridged two creeks distant one or two miles from here.

Mr Hobson was anxiously expected back. The last of the bread was eaten at dinner. We have nothing left but beef.

'26.5.1844. The first Sunday that we have camped. Bennett read the service to our own family. The men were all busy bridging creeks further on, the gents in looking after the cattle. Mr Reoch counted the cattle this morning and found that 100 of the original number were short. A great many, no doubt, were left behind in the thick scrubs we passed through. Some were obliged to be left from being too weak to travel. We have not seen a bit of grass in the past fortnight — nothing but stunted scrub for the cattle to eat.

I forgot to mention in the proper place, when Mr — went back with the blackman, Bonny, to look for Mr Hobson's horse, Mr — picked up a knife. When talking to the black he said "Dropped by a white man, I believe". He re-plied . . ." No. It was left some months ago by ??? (two other blacks of the same tribe) and myself when we came to kill some Gipps Land blacks" (with whom they are always hostile). He went on to state that they had fallen in with nine men women and children and had killed every one of them and that the knife Mr — had picked up was the same that they had cut them up with (a thing they always do with their enemies. They have a most revolting custom, that of eating the fat. It is from some superstitious notion that they have). Mr _____ examined the knife and found blood on it.

A few days previous, Bonny took great pains to explain the whole affair to me when we were passing near the spot but I did not pay much attention to it at the time.

Eight o'clock Mr Hobson returned, accompanied by Mr Brodribb and Mr Tom. A man was instantly despatched to the boat for some flour and butter they had brought with them. Some cakes were soon made and we had a good supper of bread and butter, the first we had for three weeks.'

The very long entry for Sunday, 26 May 1844, is apparently the last in the diary. Does this mean that Hazel Bennett went down to Port Albert on the boat? We know that she and her family reached the Hazelwood area and lived there for some years. Is there another diary waiting to be discovered? Was there another diary thrown away years ago, or perhaps locked in some dusty drawer?

It seems a shame that the name of Hazelwood was changed more than a hundred years later to honour a man who, however great he was, had never set foot in the Latrobe Valley and had done nothing to help develop Gippsland. At least the Morwell Historical Society has helped to ensure that Hazel Bennett will not be forgotten. Here is almost the only female voice recorded from that part of our history.

55 Ned Stringer, Mountain Man

On the roadside near Toongabbie there is a sign which points the way to Ned Stringer's grave. Yet little is known of this extraordinary mountain man and pioneer, explorer and prospector, who is remembered as the man who found gold where Walhalla now stands, though he was not alone in the discovery.

When the Jericho goldfield on the Jordan River, south of Woods Point, was opened up in the early 1860s the merchants of East Gippsland saw that there was a potentially profitable outlet for their goods in the new settlement. Immediately they began to press for a road to be built up into the hills from the south side. Until this was done the area was supplied from the Goulburn Valley to the north and the Government was opening up a route from the west through Healesville and the Yarra Valley.

The merchants found their track and soon goods began to flow to the goldfields from the south. Most supplies came from Melbourne to Port Albert by sea and were then taken by road to Sale and by pack horse into the hills.

This drive by the storekeepers created more interest in the southern slopes of the Great Divide and soon there was barely a creek which was not being prospected. Many of these yielded gold but only a few yielded enough to be called profitable and even fewer ever made a prospector wealthy.

In November 1862, one group of prospectors decided to look elsewhere. They were Edward Stringer, William Thompson, William Griffiths and William McGregor. Stringer was the leader, apparently because he was the most capable bushman in the party.

The party worked its way down the Thompson River to a point about thirteen kilometres south of Walhalla but they had little luck.

They then decided to return to a small creek they had seen earlier and they prospected their way up this for about three kilometres. There they found, at the junction of the east and west branches, several payable patches of alluvial gold. This was a couple of days after Christmas 1862, and Walhalla was about to be born.

No time could be wasted by the party. The Government offered rewards to the discoverers of workable goldfields but these were paid to the first to report the field, not always the original discoverer. The claim had to filed, in any case, to protect the rights of the four men. After all, a claim belonged legally to the man who first registered it, whether he was the finder or not.

Stringer left the camp on 12 January, by which time they had mapped out the best deposits. He was suffering from dysentery and it took him four days to reach the nearest mining registrar and lodge the claim. The registrar allowed the party 1280 metres of the creek bed and Stringer was back in camp on 18 January. The registrar was at Bald Hills (Seaton, near Glenmaggie) so the trip was a fairly fast one for a sick man in country where there were no real tracks.

For some reason Stringer mentioned the find when passing Fultons Creek. This was strange act, because there was immediately a rush to 'Stringer's creek' and the original party was only able to hold on to about 366 metres of the 1280 metre claim.

The settlement that was to become Walhalla was off to a roaring start.

The three partners who had worked with Stringer fade out of view at this point, but Ned continued to live and work on the creek for a short time. Both the creek and the settlement bore his name for several years.

The question remains. Who, exactly, was Ned Stringer? There is no single answer. He was a thief and a hero, a policeman and a convict, a chimney sweep and a prospector. He lived under several names and his true story will probably never be fully known.

The Cheshire Assizes of 28 July 1841 saw one Edward Stringer tried for burglary and theft. Found guilty, he was sentenced to be transported to Van Diemens Land for ten years. He had already had convictions for assault. The *Triton* landed him in Hobart on 19 December 1842. He was then a single man of twenty-three years, a chimney-sweep by trade and of no particular distinction in appearance. He was given nineteen months of probationary labour in the colony before being transferred to the Rocky Hills probationary centre in August 1844.

In November he was granted a ticket of leave and became a constable. He lasted as a constable for less than a month and was then dismissed from the constabulary and sentenced to two months hard labour for allowing two prisoners to escape. Stringer appealed unsuccessfully and found himself back on the wrong side of the bars.

He received a conditional pardon on 27 November 1849. At this time he apparently decided to make a fresh start and crossed from Van Diemens Land to the Port Phillip District. There is no official record of him from then until the registering of his claim in 1862, even under his two known aliases. For some reason best known to himself he went at times under the names of Edward Randel (which was apparently his real name because his birth certificate, signed at Lancaster in 1819, uses it) and Edward Macklesfield.

In September 1863, only ten months after the discovery of the alluvial gold deposits, he set out for Sale to visit a doctor. He had been troubled by a persistent cough which was steadily becoming worse. On 29 September on the way back to his claim, he stayed the night at Toongabbie. There he had a coughing fit which was so severe that he burst a blood vessel and died of the resulting haemorrhage. A party of diggers left the diggings immediately they heard the news and went down to Toongabbie, where they accorded him a solemn and sorrowful funeral. He was buried by the roadside but the Rosedale Council had his remains transferred to the Toongabbie Cemetery in 1885.

He died before the Government approved the reward for his find. McGregor and Griffiths each received £100. Thompson got nothing because he apparently left the prospecting party just before the actual discovery. The share that was Stringer's was to go to his relatives. He was known to have had a father, brother and three sisters living in Staffordshire but I have found no record of the money ever having found its way to them.

Whatever his crimes may have been, when Ned Stringer found gold in his panning dish one day in the deep hills in 1862, he paid his debt to society in full.

56 Koo Wee Rup – the Story of a Beginning

Koo Wee Rup is an Aboriginal name which is popularly supposed to mean 'blackfish swimming'. It was once known as Yallock, which was one of the words for 'creek'. Either name would have been singularly appropriate.

The dark and dismal Great Swamp, later known as the Koo Wee Rup Swamp, was one of the great obstacles to the development of Gippsland. It was a vast area of ti-tree swamp stretching from Cranbourne to Longwarry and from Western Port to the Princes Highway. Now it represents one of the great Australian success stories in land development. When much of it was included in the great Western Port Stations complex of Mickle, Bakewell and Lyall, the three despaired of it ever being drained. Falkingham, the contractor who built that stage of the railway into South Gippsland, ran into enormous difficulties crossing the swamp. Much of his line had to be carried on bridges, so that he was eighteen months late completing his contract.

Still, it was this railway which really gave Koo Wee Rup its beginning. In 1889 it was carrying goods and passengers to Yallock, though it was not formally opened until 11 November 1890. At that time Yallock was little more than a tent-town, serving the railway. The coming of the railway and the draining of the swamp gave Koo Wee Rup the chance to grow but the population was still only 500 in 1920 and only 650 in 1950. Even now, it is little more than 1,000.

The drains were as important as the railway. The most important is undoubtedly the Main Drain, which is more or less (in winter it is more, in summer it is less) the Bunyip River. This drain was suggested in 1888 by the Public Works Department engineer W. Thwaites. It has a catchment area of more than 1166 square kilometres.

Work on the drain began in May 1889, and by October 1892 it was fifteen kilometres long. The surveyors worked from flat-bottomed boats and often had to fell trees to get a firm footing for their instruments. The drain proved to be a valuable source of extra income for farmers and unemployed workers.

In 1893 the engineer in charge, Carlo Catani, decided that drainage works had proceeded far enough to allow settlers to begin taking up the land. He instituted a village settlement scheme under which workers on the drains were able to take up land cheaply, provided they maintained a laid-down scale of improvements to their properties. One such settlement was called 'Kooweerup' and was about eight kilometres north-east of the present town.

Later that year the swamp was subjected to twice the amount of rainfall that engineer Thwaites had said would cause 'extraordinary floods', and it did. The flood which followed was extraordinary enough for all concerned. The settlers who had come in under Catani's scheme were ruined. The drain was proven to be almost totally inadequate, so between 1894 and 1896 it was deepened and widened.

A second attempt was made at settlement at the 'five-mile' where the peat country began. This eventually became Koo Wee Rup North. A government store was set up to provide tools and other supplies, at a reasonable charge. This was in November 1894. At this time the settlement had a pay office (for the drainage workers), a general store, a government store and a blacksmiths.

There was bad blood between the government and the private stores. The settlers under Catani's scheme were required to buy all their tools from the government store and were actively encouraged to buy on credit, against their pay. The private store could not afford to extend much credit at all.

At the end of 1894 the Bunyip River was diverted into the Main Drain. At the same time the land at Yallock was being divided into lots of eight hectares each as the drainage took effect. In 1895 there was enough cleared and drained land for each settler to be given a grant sufficient to purchase one cow.

In 1897 a creamery was opened on a co-operative basis at the junction of the Yallock Creek and the Yallock No. 5 Drain. This had a rather chequered career and was eventually taken over by the Lang Lang Butter Factory. This creamery was a great boon to the earliest settlers but was of little use to the settlers at the 'five-mile' and in Koo Wee Rup itself.

In 1897 the drainage was finished, having cost £185,000, more than twice the estimated cost. In 1898, by a supreme irony, having for a time answered their 'trial by flood' the farmers faced a 'trial by fire'. Fences, homes and sheds were burnt. The peat beneath the surface caught fire and burned for months. Many of the roads were unsafe because of the smouldering peat beneath them. The bushfire was then followed by a period of drought which caused great hardship and a clamour for — of all things — irrigation! On the Great Swamp!

The fires had destroyed many farmers' hopes but they also cleared a great deal of land and saved the farmers some of their projected costs. At this time many of the settlers switched to mixed farming, planting potatoes and running a dairy herd. Farm sizes were increased as farmers took up abandoned properties and consolidated them with their own. It was this consolidation which made the farms viable at last.

In 1900 the swamp flooded again and the settlers were offered piece-work on upgrading the existing drains and building new ones. This had been planned earlier but was postponed because of the fear of fire in the dried-out peat along the banks. Things began to look more hopeful for the farmers again but 1901 saw an even greater flood. Koo Wee Rup East, a newly settled area, was flooded to a depth of almost two metres. Potato and onion crops were destroyed and many cattle were drowned. The settlers were 'back to square one'. However, they persisted, and in the coming decade most of them became safely established and built up reserves against the difficult times that all farmers face.

One has to admire the tenacity and the determination to 'own their own places' that kept these men going through flood after flood, fire and drought.

57 Koo Wee Rup—The Continuation

The drainage schemes and the coming of the railway made a vast difference to the Koo Wee Rup Swamp. Most of the towns on the swamp were directly affected by both events. Clyde grew up around the railway station and the original settlement became Clyde North. At Tooradin, though there was some resentment at the distance of the station from the town, the fishermen were at least able to rail their catch direct to Melbourne instead of taking it across to Hastings.

The Yallock settlement, which was to become Koo Wee Rup, grew up around the railway station. The area on which the town grew was part of a property originally belonging to a settler named Moody, after whom Moodys Inlet was named. The survey was carried out in 1889 and a site of fourteen hectares was reserved for the town in June of that year. There were already people living there, of course, including a Mrs Hudson who had built a large house called 'The Grange' on Rossiters Road in 1888.

The town allotments were sold on 15 March 1890, but Koo Wee Rup took a long time to grow. The continued struggles of the farmers and settlers against droughts, fires and annual floods seemed to put a real damper on development. John O'Riordan came from Yarra Glen in 1890 to open a store. In 1900 he opened another and obtained a wine and spirits licence which he held until the Royal Hotel was opened in 1915.

For some reason the Koo Wee Rup Swamp has always had a high proportion of Roman Catholics and this was true of the embryo township. The first church in Koo Wee Rup belonged to the Presbyterians but the Catholics built the first 'proper church' and opened it on 24 August 1902. At this time Koo Wee Rup was under the care of Father Burn of Dandenong. In 1905 it became part of the parish of Iona, and St John's School was opened in 1906.

The Presbyterians met at 'The Grange' on 21 January 1896, and organised a fund-raising drive to pay for a church building, Christopher Moody donated land in Rossiter Street and the Wesleyan Church building in Cranbourne was bought for £70. Another £25 was spent in moving it to Koo Wee Rup. A service was held in March 1896, and regular services began in September. This building was used by the Anglicans and the Methodists as well, the Anglican Minister being the Reverend H. Hitchcock. He conducted the first Anglican service in Koo Wee Rup on 7 October 1897, but St George's Church of England was not built until 1915.

State School No. 2629, Koo Wee Rup, was opened on 1 November 1884. It was built about five-kilometres to the east of the present township at the corner of Bayles and Bethune Roads. At that time it was called the Yallock school, becoming Koo Wee Rup in 1903 and being shifted into the township in 1911.

State School No. 3198, Koo Wee Rup North, was originally called Koo Wee Rup South and was built to serve some of the village settlement scheme people. It was brought from San Remo and another building was brought from Bloomfield (Nilma) to serve as a residence. Schools were almost as portable in those days as they are now!

Modella school was originally named Koo Wee Rup East but was eventually named for the property on which it was built, part of Modella Park. Cora Lynn State School was known as Koo Wee Rup Central from its opening on 1 January 1907, until September of the same year. The Higher Elementary School did not come into being until 1953 and became a High School in 1957.

The first public hall was built in 1902; this was followed by a Bush Nursing Hospital in 1910. The recreation ground was formally proclaimed in 1907 and the English, Scottish and Australian Bank opened a branch in Koo Wee Rup in 1908.

Between 1900 and 1910 and again in the 1920s, Koo Wee Rup grew fairly quickly and at the same time Lang Lang and Cranbourne began to stagnate. This may well have been due to the electrification of the line to Dandenong and the growth of the Dandenong market. Both of these led to the development of Dandenong as a regional centre and lessened the need for other centres. Retail services in Dandenong boomed at the same time.

Why Koo Wee Rup was spared the decline of other towns nearby is not quite clear. The difference in fortunes led, however, to a move in 1923 to shift the municipal headquarters from Cranbourne to Koo Wee Rup which, after some very heated debate, was defeated. Part of the reason for the failure of the move might have been the bad floods in October 1923, and August 1924. These at least gave people something else to think about! In 1934 and again in 1937, while talks on new drainage schemes were still in progress, the town was inundated. There were minor floods in 1935 but the people of Koo Wee Rup were too used to floods by now to worry about minor flooding. It was just part of the annual routine.

In 1915 work had begun on the railway branch line to Strzelecki and this made Koo Wee Rup a rail junction until 1959 and brought it a little more prosperity than it might otherwise have enjoyed. Now Koo Wee Rup goes about its business in a quietly confident way, but none of the older families have forgotten that the town owes its existence to those first settlers who simply refused to be driven from their land by flood, fire or drought.

58 Puffing Billy Rides Again

Puffing Billy is the survivor of a proud era in the railroad history of Victoria. The narrow-gauge railways were not mere tourist attractions when they were first opened. Instead, they were a means of bringing development to the remote parts of the hill country beyond the reach of the more expensive broad-gauge lines.

The smaller trains of the narrow-gauge could operate in terrain where it was impossible or uneconomic to construct the earthworks for the heavier and more costly broad-gauge trains. They could still haul considerable loads, as Puffing Billy proves as he hauls huge crowds through the hills to Emerald.

The first of these 'mini-lines' (apart from the timber tramways) was the line up the King River valley from Wangaratta to Whitfield. It was expected that this line would extend into the hills beyond, where the larger trains could not operate. Improved road transport made this unnecessary and the line closed in 1953.

The next to be built was the Gembrook line Puffing Billy uses. Then, in 1902 another narrow-gauge line was built between Colac and Beech Forest and in 1911 it was extended deeper into the Otway Ranges to terminate at Crowes. The line had a total length of more than sixty-four kilometres, making it the longest of all the narrow-gauge routes in Victoria. I can remember my excitement at riding on it during a Boy Scouts' exercise in the early 1960s.

On 15 March 1910, the residents of Walhalla turned out in force (they could, in those days!) to welcome their first train. The Walhalla line left the main Gippsland line at Moe and ran across flat dairying country for several kilometres before it entered the hills and the benefit of the narrow-gauge became obvious. It then wound and twisted its way to Erica, across the Thompson River and up into the Stringers Creek gully towards Walhalla. It was borne on a series of trestles and brackets that represented a major feat of engineering, and it is more than just a pity that the small group of enthusiasts who have been struggling to re-open part of the line have been blocked by a combination of individual selfishness and Government apathy. By 1954 the line was closed and it seems unlikely that it will ever be re-opened.

The railway to Mirboo was planned as a narrow-gauge line but local residents opposed this, seeing it as being somehow second-rate. In the end, a broad-gauge line was built at a greater cost.

Puffing Billy runs, of course, on the old Gembrook line. Work began on this in 1899. Gembrook was then a rapidly-growing agricultural central and still had a substantial timber trade. The farmers raised potatoes and these, and the timber, needed cheap heavyweight transport and a railway was the obvious plan.

Various towns were considered as the starting-points, including Dandenong, Beaconsfield, Pakenham and Nar Nar Goon. Ferntree Gully was eventually chosen because there would be more people served by the line en route than if it ran through the sparsely-populated southern foothills. The line was opened on 18 December 1900 when Tank Engine No. 4 pulled a mixed train to Gembrook. The stations on the line were Monbulk, Menzies Creek, Emerald, Devon and Gembrook. Stations built later were Upwey, Tecoma, Selby, Clematis, Nobelius, Lakeside, Wright and Fielder. The Monbulk Station was later renamed Belgrave and the Devon Station became Cockatoo.

The line was almost immediately successful. Not only did it carry thousands of tonnes of timber, potatoes and general produce, and many passengers, but it was also popular with excursionists who left the city for a day in the healthy air of the hills .

At that time, a trip in the Dandenongs was quite the thing to do. Initially there were insufficient passenger cars so seats were placed in goods trucks with a canvas roof. The number of day trippers grew so much that, in 1919, new excursion carriages were provided. These had no windows but some protection from the elements was provided by canvas screens. Some of these are still in use on the train today.

The line was no rough-and-ready affair, though. The engine shed at Upper Ferntree Gully could hold six locomotives. Automatic signalling was used on the line which was one of the first in Australia to be so equipped. For years the little trains worked up and down the valley without mishap, becoming a part of the way of life of the hills.

In 1952 disaster struck without warning. There was a watering-point between Menzies Creek and Selby where the tiny locomotives could quench the thirst they had worked up during the climb from Ferntree Gully. In December 1952, just beyond this point, a landslide covered the line. This was soon cleared but it was obvious that the hillside above the line was unstable. Another landslide in August of 1953 covered the line and buried the rails more deeply than before. The Victorian Railways decided to close the line.

During December 1954 the Melbourne newspaper *The Sun* arranged for a number of school children to have a last ride on the line. This attracted such widespread support that the Victorian Railways continued to run excursion trains through into 1955. This brief reprieve allowed time for the formation of the Puffing Billy Preservation Society. Volunteer workers kept the little trains running and there were even occasions on which the line showed a profit.

Another blow was about to fall. The line to Belgrave was electrified and a large part of Billy's route was handed over to his larger cousins. On Sunday, 23 February 1958, Billy pulled his last train sadly into Belgrave. It seemed that an era had ended.

The volunteers had not given up, however. The Citizen Military Forces helped repair the landslide area. Volunteers worked all along the lineside and on the new terminus at Belgrave. Locomotives (6NA and 7NA) were obtained and, on 28 July 1962, the line was re-opened to Menzies Creek with scenes which were often highly emotional. Within ten months the line had carried 100,000 passengers and that success story is still continuing.

At Belgrave the platform has had to be extended to 116 metres to handle the increased traffic, making it one of the longest narrow-gauge railway platforms in the world. The Mount Lyell Mining and Railway Company provided four enclosed passenger coaches, these being transported to the mainland at no charge by a shipping company. The Newport workshops of the Victorian Railways carried out the necessary work on them and they went into service. Finally, on 31 July 1965, Puffing Billy came back to Emerald. Now his route has been extended to Emerald Lake.

The work of the volunteers and the organisations which have helped has had two significant effects. Firstly, a part of our heritage and a great tourist attraction has been preserved and, secondly, we have all been provided with a great example of what ordinary men and women can do when a dream motivates them to work together.

59 The Suffering of Modella

Until about 1900 Modella was a vast and impenetrable forest of black ti-tree swamp, infested with leeches and snakes. The history of settlement had begun before 1900 but those who took up the land had been able to do nothing with it. Drainage was the key to the eventual opening-up of the area.

Modella, or Koo Wee Rup East as it was then called, was officially thrown open for selection in 1900 but a large flood prevented most of the settlers who had taken up the land from moving in. Those who had done so before the flood came down were virtually ruined, and many of the would-be farmers were granted piecework on the drainage schemes to tide them over but the flood held up even that. Even when the drains were completed, excess water in the Lang Lang River and the King Parrot Creek still backed up and flooded the land between Modella and Catani. Major floods occurred again in 1911 and 1916.

Some of the families of these early settlers have become very well-known. Mr M. J. Chambers selected a block in 1902 after he returned from the Boer War. His son, Ron, is the long-serving Shire Engineer in the Shire of Pakenham; others were S. J. Rogers in 1903 and T. Martin in 1904. The latter was in the habit of riding a bicycle to Melbourne to visit his family every few weeks until he had his selection well enough prepared to bring them out. Other names to make their first appearance in the locality at this time were the Adams, the Fallons and the Linehams.

In 1906 a settler named Hughes built a small store which was also used as the post office. He used a jinker to make deliveries every second day. A contractor named Fisher built a road to Modella from Longwarry and it seems that he might have been responsible also for Fisher Road, near the Robin Hood Hotel.

The Water Commission agreed that the overflow from the Lang Lang River should be checked. They reached this decision in 1917 but there was, obviously enough, a shortage of labour at the time. After the war many soldiers took up blocks but, despite the efforts of the Water Commission, flooding was still a major problem and the new settlers threatened to walk off their blocks en masse. A huge flood in 1923 swamped the whole area, destroying potato crops and submerging the cheese factory at Cora Lynn to a depth of two metres.

The slow progress being made on the No. 6 Drain and the No. 7 Drain aggravated the tempers of the stricken farmers and a nasty situation began to arise. An inquiry in 1924 came to the conclusion that the farmers had indeed suffered badly and that only those who had taken other employment had been able to survive financially. There was little relief work available. The rains continued throughout 1924 with a total well above the annual average. A sheet of water twenty-three kilometres long covered the area to a depth of one and half metres.

In 1925 a Royal Commission decided that the area could be farmed but that a great deal of drainage work would be necessary. This was a classic example of the work of most Royal Commissions. No-one knows quite what this brilliant deduction cost the taxpayers. In any case, the next two years were drier, which helped the farmers get back on their feet and allowed the Water Commission to make some headway with the drains.

The Closer Settlement Acts of 1925 and 1928 lowered the rates of repayment facing farmers and things began to look more hopeful for them, in 1927 the next problem arose. Potato prices dropped dramatically and in 1928 the crops were hit by disease. At the same time dairy-produce prices were at a record low so there was no relief in that direction.

December 1934 saw the largest floods ever to hit the swamp. More than 1,000 people were homeless. Bridges and roads were swept away. Crops were either washed out of the ground or they rotted where they were. The earthworks of the drains were eroded and the drains were partially choked. More than 8,000 cattle were lost.

Once more the farmers had their backs to the wall. Outward traffic from Longwarry Railway Station was value at £3,300 in 1933-34 but this dropped to less than half, being about £1,400 in 1934-35. This was the last of the great floods, though, and the drains were soon more or less completed. There have been a number of small floods since, but now the drainage can usually cope with them. Because of the boggy condition farmers usually used bullocks for clearing and ploughing; horses were for transport only.

Mr Douglas brought the first tractor to Modella in about 1910. This monster was said to have weighed between eight and ten tonnes. One of the Schmutter clan had milking machines in about the same year and separators for cream were becoming more common. A Mr Wildes of Yannathan and a Mr Priestley bought motor cars in 1915. These terrified the horses they passed along the road. Apparently they sometimes terrified the drivers also, because Mr Wildes once drove his into a drain.

Mr Coury opened a general store in 1912 but Mr Hughes still had the post office. He took the mails into Longwarry to meet the early train in his jinker. This jinker doubled as a sort of unofficial taxi. In 1920 the post office was moved to Thomas Martin's place and his eldest daughter acted as the Postmistress. When she married, the next daughter took over the role and so on down the long line of the Martin daughters. Altogether the Martins ran the post office for forty-three years. The telephone was connected in the early 1920s, and by 1925 there were four homes making use of the 9.00 a.m. to 6.00 p.m. telephone exchange.

Modella was founded in conditions of great adversity. It faced enormous difficulties in becoming established and it is due to the same spirit that overcame these difficulties in the first place that Modella is still very much a community today.

60 William Lyall and 'Harewood'

The prominence of 'Harewood', set on what was once a wild and lonely moor, has made it a landmark for travellers. A hundred years ago it was a social centre for the area north of Western Port. William Lyall, who built 'Harewood', was one of the finest examples of the squatter who gave more than he took. He was industrious, imaginative, kind and intelligent, and he had all the virtues regarded as vital in the Victorian era. Perhaps the greatest attribute of all was that everything he touched seem to turn to gold!

Lyall was born in Scotland in 1821. He came with his father and three brothers to Van Diemens Land in 1835, settling on the Tamar River. He was generally regarded as a well set-up young man and was widely popular. His first business venture seems to have been shipping cattle across the Strait for sale in Melbourne.

In 1847 he was sharing a house with John Mickle (1814-1885) when his sister, Margaret Lyall, fell in love with Mickle. They were married and were very happy together. Two years later, Lyall married Annabelle Brown. By this time Mickle and Lyall had a very close friendship. The two had a third friend in John Bakewell (1807-1888) and the three young men formed a business partnership that was to endure for many years and was to shape the history of the north end of Western Port for four decades.

In 1847 Lyall began to transfer his business interests to the Port Phillip District. He and Annabelle, who was related to the great Clydebank shipbuilding family of Browns, moved to 'Stony Park' at Brunswick. They then lived in Kew for a time before moving on to their model Scottish farm, 'Frogmore', at Murrumbeena.

The three young partners next took up land in the Western District but they soon turned their attention to the Yallock run on the Great Swamp. They took up Yallock in 1851 and with it they took up Tooradin and Monomeith Stations. Tooradin was not actually purchased until 1852. It had originally been Manton's but Lyall bought it from John Pike and, in 1852, he and his wife moved into the old Manton homestead.

There were many problems in those early years but, one by one, they were overcome. Drainage and distance from the Melbourne markets were the only two which took a long time to conquer. Among lesser problems were the near-burning down of the Yallock homestead and the robbing of it by two bushrangers who were later recaptured. The gold fever affected two of William Lyall's younger brothers, John and Andrew. They and Tom Mickle had £86 to finance a trip to the diggings, but they returned a month later with no gold and no money.

Fodder was always a problem. In the summer of 1853-54 there was so little available that Lyall and Mickle went to Tasmania in the steamer *Clarence* to buy hay. They bought 303 tons at the amazing price of 4s a ton, delivered to Melbourne. The two men then turned their trip into something of a tour. They visited Hobart and the original Lyall properties in Tasmania before boarding the *Lady Bird* for the trip home. From this time on the trio really began to go ahead financially.

'Harewood' was planned as a hunting lodge as early as 1858. Lyall was a keen sportsman and naturalist and there were fish to catch and ducks and other game to hunt. However, he did not succeed in persuading Annabelle to move to 'Harewood' until 1868. Construction of the main house began in 1865 under the direction of an architect named Martelli, the builders being George Binding and Sons. The timber was for the most part brought from Dandenong, where there was a thriving sawmilling industry (mainly producing sawn red gum blocks for the paving of Melbourne streets). The redgum timber alone cost £82.

Some of the bricks were made on the property using a machine Lyall had imported from England at a cost of £300 but the variable quality of the local clay and the difficulty of hiring men who knew much about brickmaking meant that most of the bricks had to be brought around from Melbourne by ship. Small sailing vessels which could anchor in the nearby inlets were used. It is difficult to imagine just how these heavily-laden little ships could navigate the tortuous channels leading into the inlets but they did. (Another source of information claims that the brick-making machinery was not imported until 1875 and was set up to supply the bricks for 'Warrock', a few kilometres to the east).

The building is most imposing. It stands back from the South Gippsland Highway looking for all the world like something out of *Wuthering Heights*. It has a lonely grandeur, emphasised by the low outline of French Island behind it and the marshes which surround it.

There is a high-gabled central hall, once roofed with glass, in which Lyall kept tree-ferns, palms and other hot-house plants. The hall was used as a dining room when dances were held at 'Harewood'. Eventually, however, the fierce storms which occasionally swept in from the Strait, bringing hail, forced Lyall to cover-in the glass roof. The dances and social functions held at 'Harewood' were known throughout West Gippsland. Many a blushing debutante made her debut at 'Harewood', including my own great-aunts. They travelled down from Officer, taking two days to cross the swamp and camping-out along the way. Debutantes sometimes had to be hardy souls in those days, it seems.

Governor Sir George Bowen lunched at the Lyall homestead while on a shooting trip on 11 April 1877, and three days later Lyall entertained him again. Lord and Lady Hopetoun visited Mrs Lyall after her husband's death in 1888. Many other influential people were house guests at different times. It seems strange that, given the number of 'friends in high places' Lyall had, he never sought any political career. He did represent Mornington in Parliament between September 1859 and August 1861, but he never seems to have pursued the idea of politics to any great extent. Perhaps he was too busy!

Certainly he was a very popular man, loved by both the remnants of the Aboriginal tribes in the area and the most educated whites. It is said that he refused a decoration. There is no proof of this, but it would have been in character.

61 Your Guide to the Beaconsfield Ranges

In the 1890s, quite the place to go for your holidays was to Upper Beaconsfield. T. C. Mackley wrote of the Beaconsfield Ranges in 1899: 'No scene in fairy land could surpass the beauties of this southern paradise ... Various forms of wattle, whose home is in the gullies, queen of whom — she of the silver leaf — towers aloft ... shedding the fragrance of her golden blossoms through the Spring air with a lavishness that only nature knows. Under these again, in sheltered shade, runs the rippling stream . . .'

The Upper Beaconsfield Progressive League published a booklet in 1899 entitled *An Illustrated Guide To The Beaconsfield Ranges*. It sold at 6d per copy and Mackley was one of the writers. At that time the Progressive League was a very strong body, and included many members of Parliament. The whole community supported it and it was successful in obtaining many improvements for the area and the township.

The area known as the Beaconsfield Ranges during the 1890s was originally taken up as a sheep run by Messrs Bourke and Neville. It was on the northern boundary of the famous Panty Gurn Gurn Run. Beaconsfield itself was then known as Little Berwick, though it was soon to be much larger than Berwick, at least for a few years.

Mrs Bowman opened a hotel at the Cardinia Creek crossing on the Gippsland Road; another was opened a little further north at a different creek crossing. The Border Hotel in Berwick was open at the same time so thirsts acquired on the Berwick Hill could be well catered for, no matter which way the traveller was heading.

In 1870 gold was found in the hills north of Berwick and Little Berwick. The towns began to grow quite quickly; soon there were more than 200 miners working in Haunted Gully alone. Others spread throughout the hills prospecting along the many small creeks, making a number of finds which provided semi-permanent encampments.

Three years later another rush to Bendigo drew the miners away but by this time the settlement at Upper Beaconsfield (though it did not yet have a name) was permanent. Early in 1878 an amendment to the 1869 *Land Act* allowed the selection of blocks of eight hectares without any residential requirement. About 200 'city gentlemen' purchased blocks around the town, drawn by the clean air and the panoramic views.

Soon it became obvious that a railway station was needed at Little Berwick. The Oakleigh to Sale railway was open but there was no station at Cardinia Creek (which name was now as common as Little Berwick) and travellers were required to leave the train at Berwick, on the wrong side of the hill. The Honourable John Woods, Minister for Railways, was invited to a monster picnic, where the large number of people attending convinced him of the need for a station. There is a story that settlers from kilometres away were persuaded to come along and swell the crowd. The Minister asked that a deputation wait upon him in Melbourne to finalise arrangements.

J. B. Patterson, the Postmaster-General, was now pressed to provide postal and telegraph services. He agreed on the condition that the services proved profitable, which they did.

At this time a Mr Brisbane was building a guest house at Upper Beaconsfield. This huge building was officially the Beaconsfield

House Hotel but the locals always called it 'The Big House'. Unfortunately, at the turn of the century a spectacular blaze destroyed the building and it was not rebuilt. Another landmark, the great white 'Salisbury House' also dates from this period.

In 1884 a committee consisting of Messrs Halford, A'Beckett, Goff, Brind and Elms formed another committee to arrange the construction of a local hall and meeting place. By 1889 the hall stood on half a hectare of land bought from Jacques Martin, free of all debt and complete with an organ, a piano and a lending library with some thousands of volumes. The project had cost the small community £1600. A tennis court was added and another eight hectares were obtained for a cricket ground — all through local effort without subsidy or help from any outside source.

Though Upper Beaconsfield went into a decline for some years the growing pressure on land resources has brought about a considerable revival of the town. In 1974, just as in 1884, people are moving to Upper Beaconsfield to find peace and quiet, clean air and a pleasant outlook.

62 The Mirboo Railway

The Mirboo district was thrown open for selection in 1878, about four years after settlers began looking for land in the hills south of Morwell. The task they faced was a daunting one. Some of the settlers came up from the Port Albert district, working their way up the valleys of the Tarwin watershed. Settlers from Morwell had just as rugged a task. They used packhorses to take in their supplies and tools and then took the horses back because there was no feed for them in the hills until the land was cleared and sown.

Agitation for a railway soon began, for the railway was the 'kiss of life' to many small settlements before roads were developed and motor transport became fast and efficient. The carting of goods was an expensive business, with costs running as high as £8 per ton between Mirboo and the main railway. Mr Peacock of Mirboo recorded in his diary that he attended a meeting to form a Railway League on 24 April 1880. In May of that year a deputation of South

Gippsland residents waited upon the Minister for Railways to ask for a line north from Welshpool to the main Gippsland line as a means of opening up the area.

Later in 1880 the deputation again saw the Minister, this time putting forward the alternatives of line through Drouin and Poowong or from Morwell to Mirboo. On 17 October 1880, a Railway Bill presented to Parliament made provision for the construction of eighteen railways. One of these was to run south from Morwell to Mirboo. The number of railways in the Bill meant a shortage of survey teams so survey work did not actually begin until July 1881. The survey was not completed until July 1882, a period of twelve long months for the impatient settlers.

Though the country was rough at least one surveyor liked what he saw. He was W. H. Ritson who gave up surveying and took up a selection at Yinnar on what was originally the Scrubby Forest Run.

Hector Muirson was awarded the contract for the building of the first stage of the line. This represented about half of the total distance, running through fairly easy country with one station to be built, at Yinnar. He tendered the sum of £18,460 11s but before he was able to begin it was decided to let the whole job as one contract and this time he was unsuccessful. This second contract went to John S. White on 12 January 1883. He quoted the price of £74,901 6s 11d.

While there were no rock cuttings there were a considerable number of clay cuttings and embankments. Probably the biggest single problem was the lack of suitable rock for ballast. Nevertheless, construction went ahead, marked by incidents both funny and tragic: one Martin Kildare was seriously injured in an earth-fall and transport was so bad he could not be moved for four days, and a quantity of whisky was stolen in Morwell, the police being quite certain that it had been stolen to 'christen' the line.

In the early months of 1883 White ran into serious trouble. The earthworks were proving far more expensive than he had thought they would be, and he and his men were also at loggerheads over pay and conditions. There were several reports of unsatisfactory progress and White's contract was cancelled on 1 June 1883.

For a time it seemed that a horse tramway might be built instead, and the idea of a proper railway abandoned. Local citizens were aghast at this and applied considerable political pressure. In January

1884, a new contractor, John Robb, was engaged to finish the line. He was under pressure to complete the job because a new township, complete with the necessary hotel, was already growing at Mirboo. However, he was helped by the discovery of a stone deposit at Stony Creek, just west of Yinnar. A spur line about three kilometres long was built to the quarry and the ballast problem was solved.

Another town came into existence about nineteen kilometres away. This was a railway camp but it was to become Boolarra. In April of 1884 the District Inspector of Schools reported that there were thirty-two children of school age in the camp. Of these, thirty-one were from 'railway families'.

The first section of the line was opened on 10 April 1885. The station eleven kilometres out was named Yinnar and the station at the nineteen-kilometre point became Boolarra. In the same month heavy rain caused damage to some of the earthworks on the Mirboo section so that work on that section was further delayed. Robb was granted an extension of time but there were more delays. Rolling of the earth in the embankments was skimped to save time in culvert construction but this only led to further slips and problems.

On 8 September 1885, the line was opened as far as the new Darlimurla Station, twenty-six kilometres distant. The original township of Darlimurla was three kilometres away, on Lidiards Track, and this took the name of Delburn when the station was named Darlimurla.

On 1 December 1885, two and a half years after the survey began, the contractor's locomotive steamed into Mirboo for the first time. It must have been greeted with overwhelming enthusiasm by the isolated townsfolk. The formal opening took place on 7 January 1886. A special trainload of dignitaries from Melbourne and towns along the main Gippsland line were brought up and there were all the usual speeches and expressions of faith in the future. There was a huge banquet and a ball, a great many self-congratulatory toasts. Perhaps, after all, this is understandable.

In the general feeling of expansion and prosperity that prevailed there were other proposals put forward for railways. Someone suggested that a line to Yarram, beginning from Traralgon, Rosedale or Yinnar, might be a good idea. It was also thought that the Mirboo line would be only the beginning and that it would extend down into the Tarwin valley to connect the Latrobe Valley to the coast. Survey parties went in search of routes to either Welshpool or Stockyard Creek (Foster). None of these grand schemes was to come to fruition, however.

A route into South Gippsland was found, but it left the main line at Dandenong. The Mirboo line did not decay, however, as some pessimists predicted when they learnt that it was to remain only a branch line. The farmers who had fought for it were quick to use it. Timber, potatoes, butter and hay were all railed out. Passenger services were also well supported for many years.

During the coal strike in New South Wales in 1929-30 a considerable quantity of local coal was taken down the line from Mirboo, although in normal times the transportation of coal would not have been a payable proposition. Bauxite was also mined in the Mirboo North and Boolarra areas. One other product which many farmers, would rather not have been producing was rabbit carcases. The Victorian Railways shipped thousands of these from Mirboo.

The line was finally closed on 22 June 1974. It was defeated by the economies of road transport but it had served the farmers in the hills well and truly for nearly a hundred years.

63 Fish Creek and Waratah Bay

Fish Creek is an established and stable farming area. It may not seem progressive to the motorist hurrying past the Promontory Gate, one of the great traps in Gippsland, but it does have a keen sense of community.

The first settlers took up blocks around Fish Creek in the 1880s, forty years after settlement began at Welshpool, only forty-two kilometres away. The names of these first settlers have not been forgotten. They included Messrs McCartney, Falls, Synan, O'Leary, Ryan, Lawson, Buckley, Cotter, Farrell, Layer, Lowrey and Mackin. If these names sound a little Irish, who is to say that the sons of Erin were not among the bravest and the best of our pioneers?

Provisions were initially brought in from Foster by packhorse. The nearest post office was at Foster and the settlers took it in turn to go in, once a week, to collect any mail for the struggling little settlement. The mail was 'packed' down from Mirboo by John Amey, who gave his name to Ameys Track.

One of the first buildings in the present township site was the creamery. Others were Jackson's store, the Mechanics Institute, the home of Mr Lowrey (which later became the Coffee Palace) and the home of W. P. Ryan, which stood on the present school site.

An early priority was the building of a school. The first was opened in O'Leary's house in Falls Road, the schoolmaster being Joseph Yeowart. A Mr Ryan then built a small wooden schoolhouse opposite the old gravel-hopper' and this was then displaced by a more substantial structure built by Mr Synan. All this took place within one year, for Yeowart began teaching in 1890 and yet, by 10 August 1891, the Education Department was able to open a new school on Sheedy's place. Even that was temporary for in 1927 the school was moved to a site purchased from M. B. Buckley. In 1929 a building was moved from the closed Doomburrin school to Fish Creek; another was brought from Hoddle Range in 1945 when that school closed.

The first Postmaster appointed to Fish Creek was W. B. Kennedy, who ran the post office in W. P. Ryan's store. On 13 January 1892, the railway was officially opened from Korumburra to Port Albert and the post office was then conducted from the new railway station.

Fish Creek Station is, incidentally, 160 kilometres from Melbourne. It must have been the curse of many an early engineer because in the seven kilometres between Hoddle Range and Boys, as those stations were then called, the line dipped seventy-six metres and then climbed forty-four metres.

The first creamery was a co-operative enterprise, as most were, the farmers bringing their milk to the creamery on sledges. The cream was used for butter and the skimmed milk was taken home for the pigs and the calves. The creamery was later purchased by the Melbourne Chilled Butter Company which used the name 'Greenfields' on its wrappers.

Like most Gippsland towns, Fish Creek is enormously proud of and involved in its sports teams. Cricket and football have been played in the town since the days when trips to Welshpool and Tarwin Lower were made on horseback along lonely bush tracks.

The town has fielded many first-class teams and locals point proudly to a long list of premierships in several sports.

Waratah Bay is on the coast near Fish Creek and the settlers used to hold picnics at Cooks Creek, where there was always fresh water. In the last quarter of the nineteenth century Waratah Bay became busy with the shipping to and from the lime kilns. These lime deposits were discovered in about 1875 by William Millar of Yanakie Station. He gained the interest of the shipping agents, Bright Brothers. These agents built the lime kilns, the massive brickworks which are still visible on the beach at Walkerville. The first shipment was loaded aboard a small steamer, the *Blackboy*, which caught fire and was destroyed before reaching Melbourne.

Waratah Bay has not been kind to shipping. There have been at least ten large vessels lost in the area. I have even heard of the 'Ghost of Walkerville', said by some to be the wife of a captain lost in the bay. I have friends who swear they have seen her.

The lime kilns employed up to seventy men at times but the advent of cement as a building material spelt the beginning of the end. In 1926 the kilns had become so uneconomical that they had to be closed. Walkerville was, by the way, named after Mr W. F. Walker who was Commissioner of Customs in 1880 and owned one of the kilns for a time. It was originally named Waratah but that name is now used for an area about six kilometres east along the beach.

Further east is Sandy Point, for many years the quiet home of the Pilkingtons and others but now a popular resort, possessing what is quite possibly Victoria's best beach. It is surprising to find such a beautiful area, so close to Melbourne, still comparatively unspoilt.

64 Jindivick

The Old Sale Road is a well-known part of Gippsland's history. Few people realise, however, that there were other tracks to the east long before the Old Sale Road was surveyed and cleared. In about 1862 William Jackson blazed a track from the Bunyip River, near Labertouche, through the foothills north of the present Princes Highway. This track was an established cattle route many years before the Old Sale Road existed.

Jacksons Track, as it is still called, was one of two routes north of the Old Sale Road in this particular area. One was the Telegraph Road which headed east from the Bunyip River just a little north of the Tarween, now the Tarago River. This route was the more popular of the two because it was more direct. The track Jackson marked out was rather steep in places and gradually lost favour.

When the Sale Road was surveyed due east up the Picnic Point Hill and past the new coaching house, the Robin Hood, and thence out toward Brandy Creek, both Jacksons Track and the Telegraph Road fell into comparative disuse. The new road was not as steep as its predecessors and it was a little shorter. Later, the railway created new growth south of the Sale Road and yet another road east was begun. This new road became the Princes Highway and it leaves the route of the Sale Road at the Robin Hood. This junction was once known as Drouin West and before that it was Whisky Creek. Drouin West is now a little further up the Old Sale Road. Names can be portable things at times!

However, Jacksons Track was still fairly important for some years. It was sixty metres wide in places and there was less traffic to interfere with moving cattle. There are still people alive who can remember mobs of cattle coming out of Gippsland and using Jacksons Track.

David Brown wrote in his memoirs in 1923 that he had stayed at an 'accommodation house' run by the Leeson family at Cannibal Creek. It was at this point that the Telegraph Road left the main road. From there Brown travelled to the new Bunyip Hotel. The old one was still standing on the Telegraph Road about eight kilometres to the north. This would serve as some sort of proof that the Telegraph Road followed the telegraph line well to the north, as its name implies.

The original Bunyip Hotel was on the Labertouche Creek at its junction with the Bunyip River and the proprietor at the time was David de Vinny. This was in 1872.

From about 1865 Jacksons Track, which leaves the Princes Highway at Longwarry North, was used by miners heading for Crossover and the small alluvial goldfields along the foothills. It was not until the early 1870s that settlers began to seek land in the area. This was when Jindivick was born. The first recorded land sale in Jindivick was in 1878 when Robert Ireland sold 320 acres to James

Cruickshank at the high price of £4 per acre. Ten years later the land was selling at £15 and £20 per acre.

Other early land sales were to Peter Mitchell, whose descendants are still on the land, at £17 15s per acre and to Reginald Noyes at £8 10s. At first, farming in the district was mixed, with pigs being the most common livestock. One settler named Wieland had a herd of 200 pigs. When these were ready for market they were driven to Dandenong on foot.

The Jacksons, surveyors of the track which bears their name, also settled in Jindivick and were probably the first permanent settlers to do so. William Jackson had four or five sons and a daughter. They arrived in 1869 (where was he for the seven years after he blazed the track?) when William Junior was about seven years old. This lad attended the school when it opened in 1877.

Young William married the daughter of another settler named Hutchison. The daughter of this marriage married one of the Palmers, so there is still Jackson blood in the Jindivick district today.

Other names to appear in local surveys were those of Mason, Hutchison, Perschack, Gleeson, Palmer, Ramsden, Notman and Holt. Most of these were part of the new wave of settlers who moved into Gippsland as agriculturalists rather than pastoralists. That is to say, they farmed the land, clearing it and planting crops and pasture, rather than simply grazing cattle on the native herbage. It was these settlers who ensured the permanence of young settlements .

Clearing the bush was no easy task. It was necessary to clear a minimum of over four hectares a year to retain legal right to the selections. The forest consisted of tall mountain ash forest with no understory. On the face of it the technique used for clearing was simple but it involved a staggering amount of physical work. The forest was first burnt and then the logs and branches which survived were piled up for later burning. Grass seed was then scattered on top of the ashes between the still-standing tree trunks: These were removed later, when the selection was in production and there was time for 'proper' clearing. The first aim was get the land into production so that the settler didn't have to live on his limited capital.

One settler, an old man named Carroll, was caught in the fire he lit and his charred bones were found some time later. It was often a lonely life for a settler and sometimes a lonely death.

Jindivick was becoming quite settled by the turn of the century. Isaac Ramsden had given land for a school which was built in 1877. The building was a 'portable' which served until 1910 and was then replaced with a building brought from Neerim by Lee Palmer. The new building had been the old Neerim school but it was too small for Neerim's population. Attendance at the Jindivick school was always fairly stable — there were forty pupils when it opened and there were still only forty-six in 1914.

The first church was the Church of England, which opened in 1882. The building was of weatherboard and was built by Andrew Lawson of Drouin; the site was land again given by Isaac Ramsden and a Miss Lucy Ramsden was the first bride to be married in the church. The building was moved to its present site in 1910. The Presbyterians held services in the Anglican church from about 1890 and built their own church in 1910.

The Jindivick Hall was built in 1886 by a contractor named James Whitten who had selected land nearby. Since then it has been added to twice. The hall was the focus of the 'Back to Jindivick' celebrations in 1936.

A Progress Association was formed in 1908 and has been very active in accelerating the development of services in the area. Its first big campaign was for the provision of telephone services in 1911; it was also active in having another line put through to the Rokeby Station. Two electric street lamps were put up in Jindivick in 1910, for until then the only lighting was hand-lit each night. In 1923 the Progress Association began the fight for a proper electricity supply. This was at the beginning of the Yallourn power generation and transmission scheme. It was to be a long fight, for electricity was not connected to Jindivick until 1938.

Jindivick is now one of those rural settlement typical of much of Gippsland. It has a solid tradition of community self-help and little prospect of any great change.